Rick Steves ®
SNAPSHOT

Italy's Cinque Terre

CONTENTS

INTRODUCTION

This Snapshot guide, excerpted from my guidebook *Rick Steves' Italy*, introduces you to my favorite stretch of the Italian Riviera. The Cinque Terre—literally "five lands"—is a charm bracelet of picturesque, traffic-free villages where you can melt into small-town Italy. Sit on the breakwater to enjoy the views, hike the scenic trails between the villages, and dine on a succulent seafood feast as you hear the roar of the surf. I've also included coverage of nearby Riviera destinations, including the beach towns of Levanto, Sestri Levante, the larger Santa Margherita Ligure, trendier Portofino, resorty Portovenere, and the workaday transportation hub of La Spezia.

To help you have the best trip possible, I've included the following topics in this book:

• **Planning Your Time,** with advice on how to make the most of your limited time

• **Orientation,** including tourist information (abbreviated as TI), tips on public transportation, local tour options, and helpful hints

• **Sights** with ratings:

▲▲▲—Don't miss

▲▲—Try hard to see

▲—Worthwhile if you can make it

No rating—Worth knowing about

• **Sleeping** and **Eating,** with good-value recommendations in every price range

• **Connections,** with tips on trains, buses, and driving

Practicalities, near the end of this book, has information on money, phoning, hotel reservations, transportation, and more, plus Italian survival phrases.

To travel smartly, read this little book in its entirety before you go. It's my hope that this guide will make your trip more meaningful and rewarding. Traveling like a temporary local, you'll get the absolute most out of every mile, minute, and dollar.

Buon viaggio!

Rick Steves

THE CINQUE TERRE

The Cinque Terre (CHINK-weh TAY-reh), a remote chunk of the Italian Riviera, is the traffic-free, lowbrow, underappreciated alternative to the French Riviera. There's not a museum in sight—just sun, sea, sand (well, pebbles), wine, and pure, unadulterated Italy. Enjoy the villages, swimming, hiking, and evening romance of one of God's great gifts to tourism. For a home base, choose among five *(cinque)* villages, each of which fills a ravine with a lazy hive of human activity—calloused locals, sunburned travelers, and no Vespas. While the Cinque Terre is now discovered (and can be unpleasantly crowded midday, when tourist boats and cruise-ship excursions drop by), I've never seen happier, more relaxed tourists.

This chunk of coast was first described in medieval times as "the five lands." In the feudal era, this land was watched over by castles. Tiny communities grew up in their protective shadows, ready to run inside at the first hint of a Turkish Saracen pirate raid. Marauding pirates from North Africa were a persistent problem until about 1400. Many locals were kidnapped and ransomed or sold into slavery, and those who remained built fires on flat-roofed watchtowers to relay warnings—alerting the entire coast to imminent attacks. The last major raid was in 1545.

As the threat of pirates faded, the villages prospered, catching fish and cultivating grapes. Churches were enlarged with a growing population. But until the advent of tourism in this generation, the towns remained isolated. Even today, traditions survive, and each of the five villages comes with a distinct dialect and its own proud heritage.

Sadly, a few ugly, noisy Americans give tourism a bad name

The Cinque Terre

To A-12 Autostrada
(Brugnato Exit)

To
Genoa

A-12

SP-1

To
La Spezia
& Pisa

To A-12 Autostrada
(Carrodano Exit)

SP-566

To
Sestri Levante,
Santa Margherita
& Genoa

SP-370

Levanto

To New Town
(Fegina)

To Monterosso's
Old Town

SP-38

2 Kilometers

2 Miles

Beverino

Pignone

Pian di
Barca

SP-1

SP-1

SP-63

These roads likely closed.
Inquire locally.

To
La Spezia
& A-12

Monterosso
al Mare

SANDY
BEACH

Vernazza

5

4

Corniglia

3

SP-51

Volastra

CORNIGLIA STATION

Manarola

2

VIA DELL'AMORE ♥

VIA
LITORANEA

To
La Spezia
& A-12

Ligurian

Sea

Riomaggiore

1

SP-370

To Portovenere

here. Even hip, young residents are put off by loud, drunken tourists. They say—and I agree—that the Cinque Terre is an exceptional place. It deserves a special dignity. Party in Viareggio or Portofino, but be mellow in the Cinque Terre. Talk softly. Help keep it clean. In spite of the tourist crowds, it's still a real community, and we are its guests.

In this chapter, I cover the five towns in order from south to north—from Riomaggiore to Monterosso. Since I still get the names of the towns mixed up, I think of them by number: #1 Riomaggiore (a workaday town), #2 Manarola (picturesque), #3 Corniglia (on a hilltop), #4 Vernazza (the region's cover girl, the most touristy and dramatic), and #5 Monterosso al Mare (the closest thing to a beach resort of the five towns).

Arrival in the Cinque Terre

By Train: Most big, fast trains from elsewhere in Italy speed right past the Cinque Terre. (There are some exceptions: A few IC trains go directly from Milan to Monterosso and from Pisa to La Spezia and Monterosso). Unless you're coming from a nearby town, you'll most likely have to change trains at least once to reach Manarola, Corniglia, or Vernazza.

Generally, if you're coming from the north, you'll change trains in Sestri Levante or Genoa (specifically, Genoa's Piazza Principe station). If you're coming from the south or east, you'll probably have to switch trains in La Spezia (change at La Spezia Centrale station—don't make the mistake of getting off at La Spezia Migliarina). No matter where you're coming from, it's best to check in the station before you leave to see your full schedule and route options (use the computerized kiosks or ask at a ticket window). Don't forget to validate your ticket by stamping it in the green-and-white machines located on train platforms and elsewhere in the station. Conductors here are notorious for levying stiff fines on forgetful tourists. For more information on riding the train between Cinque Terre towns, see "Getting Around the Cinque Terre," later.

By Car: If you're driving in the Cinque Terre (but, given the narrow roads and lack of parking, I wouldn't), see "Cinque Terre Connections" at the end of this chapter for directions. For parking, see the "By Car" sections in each village.

Planning Your Time

The ideal stay is two or three full days; my recommended minimum stay is two nights and a completely uninterrupted day. The Cinque Terre is served by local trains from Genoa and La Spezia. Speed demons arrive in the morning, check their bags in La Spezia, ride a train to their starting point, take the five-hour hike through all five towns, laze away the afternoon on the beach or rock of their choice, and zoom away on a high-speed evening or overnight train to somewhere back in the real world. But be warned: The Cinque Terre has a strange way of messing up your momentum. (The evidence is the number of Americans who have fallen in love with the region and/or one of its residents...and are still here.) Frankly, staying fewer than two nights is a mistake that you'll likely regret.

The towns are just a few minutes apart by hourly train or boat. There's no checklist of sights or experiences—just a hike, the towns themselves, and your fondest vacation desires. Study this chapter in advance and piece together your best day, mixing hiking, swimming, trains, and a boat ride. For the best light, coolest temperatures, and fewest crowds, start your hike early.

Market days perk up the towns from 8:00 to 13:00 on Tuesday in Vernazza, Wednesday in Levanto, Thursday in Monterosso and Sestri Levante, and Friday in La Spezia.

The winter is really dead—most hotels and some restaurants close from about January to March. The long Easter weekend (April 18-21 in 2014), May, June, and September are the peak of peak periods—the toughest times to find rooms. July (when the heat keeps away many potential hikers) and August (vacation time hasn't started yet) can be surprisingly light. In spring, the towns can feel inundated with Italian school groups day-tripping on spring excursions (they can't afford to sleep in this expensive region).

For more information on the region, see www.cinqueterre.it.

Cinque Terre Park Cards

Visitors hiking between the towns on coastal trails need to pay a park entrance fee. You have three options: the Cinque Terre Park Card, the Cinque Terre Treno Park Card, and the Cinque Terre Park Card Blu. All are valid until midnight on the expiration date. Write your name on your card or risk a big fine. The configuration and pricing of these cards seem to always be in flux—be aware that the following details may change before your visit. Those under 18 or over 70 get a discount, as do families of four or more (see www. parconazionale5terre.it).

The **Cinque Terre Park Card** costs €6 for one day of hiking or €9.70 for two days (covers trails and shuttle buses but not trains, buy at trailheads and at most train stations, no validation required).

The **Cinque Terre Treno Park Card** covers what the Cinque Terre Park Card does, plus the use of the local trains (from Levanto to La Spezia, including all Cinque Terre towns). It's sold at TIs inside train stations, but not at trailheads (€12/1 day, €23/2 days, validate card at train station by punching it in the machine). With this card, you have to hike and take three train trips every day to break even.

The **Cinque Terre Park Card Blu,** tentatively planned for 2014, would cover trails, trains, and also boats connecting the towns (at least €25/1 day). This pass won't pay for itself unless you take lots of boats (that is, hiking from one end of the Cinque Terre to the other, and then riding a boat all the way back).

Getting Around the Cinque Terre

Within the Cinque Terre, you can connect towns in three ways: by train, boat, or foot. Trains are cheaper, boats are more scenic, and hiking lets you enjoy more pasta. From a practical point of view, you should consider supplementing the often frustrating trains with the sometimes more convenient boats. The Via dell'Amore trail between Riomaggiore and Manarola is a delight and takes just a few minutes (if it's open), making the train not worth waiting for.

By Train

By train, the five towns are just a few minutes apart. Along the

Events in the Cinque Terre in 2014

For more festival information and to confirm dates, check www.cinqueterre.it and www.turismoinliguria.it. The food festivals in particular are subject to change.

April 20-21	All towns: Easter Sunday and Monday
April 25	All towns: Italian Liberation Day (stay away from the Cinque Terre this day, as locals literally shut down the trails)
May 1	All towns: Labor Day (another local holiday that packs the place mostly with day-trippers)
Mid-May	Monterosso: Lemon Festival (usually the third Sunday)
May 29	All towns: Ascension Day
May 30	Monterosso and Vernazza: Feast of Corpus Domini (procession on carpet of flowers at 18:00)
Mid-June	Monterosso: Anchovy Festival
June 24	Riomaggiore and Monterosso: Feast day of St. John the Baptist (procession and fireworks; big fire on Monterosso's old town beach the day before)
June 29	Corniglia: Feast day of Sts. Peter and Paul
July 20	Vernazza: Feast day of patron saint, St. Margaret, with fireworks
Early Aug (first Sun)	Vernazza: Feast of Nostra Signora di Reggio (hike up to Reggio Sanctuary for food and church procession)
Aug 10	Manarola: Feast day of patron saint, St. Lawrence
Aug 14	Monterosso: Fireworks on eve of feast of the Assumption
Aug 15	All towns: Feast of the Assumption (Ferragosto)
Mid-Sept	Monterosso: Anchovies and Olive Oil Festival (usually the second weekend)

coast here, trains go in only two directions: *"per* [to] *Genova"* (the Italian spelling of Genoa), northbound; or *"per La Spezia,"* southbound.

Tickets: Most rides within the region cost €2.10. These tickets are good for 75 minutes in one direction, so you could conceivably use one for a brief stopover. (A short hop between very nearby towns—such as Monterosso-Vernazza or Riomaggiore-

The Cinque Terre National Park: Peaks and Valleys

Founded in 1999, the Cinque Terre National Marine Park was designed to get everyone thinking creatively about how to improve the area for the good of nature, the local communities, and its many visitors. The park designation has brought with it plenty of good things: money (in the form of trail fees), new regulations to protect wildlife, park-sponsored information centers at each train station, shuttle buses to help hikers reach distant trailheads, and improved walkways, trails, beaches, breakwaters, and docks.

But, perhaps predictably, the system has been corrupted by power and money. A charismatic and visionary past park president, nicknamed "The Pharaoh," made great inroads before poisoning the process with cronyism, forcing him to leave office in disgrace. Frequent landslides have cut off trails—the main reason many people come here—and the trails are repaired and reopened with excruciating slowness. Local grassroots movements (including Save Vernazza—see page 45—and a ragtag crew of Manarolans who donated their time to clear a scenic trail) have arguably done more to promote and preserve the Cinque Terre than has the park, even with its substantial budget. The latest park president, a retired sea admiral, is determined to make the park work. But given this region's old-fashioned ways and recent history of bureaucratic failure, success is far from assured.

Keep in mind that the Cinque Terre is a moving target. Don't be surprised if park details (including entrance fees, shuttle buses, information desks, and so on) have changed by the time you visit.

Manarola—costs €1.80.) A 40-kilometer ticket is good for six hours in one direction (€4). Buy tickets at the ticket desk or from the ticket machines on the platform. Before you board, stamp your ticket at the green-and-white machine (a Cinque Terre Treno Park Card must be validated only the first time you use it). Riding without a validated ticket can be expensive (usually €50). You can buy several tickets at once and use them as you like, validating as you go. If you have a Eurail Pass, don't spend one of your valuable travel days on the cheap Cinque Terre.

Schedule: Trains run about hourly in each direction, connecting all five towns. Frequency is a bit lower on Sundays, and more trains may be added during the busiest season (June-Sept). Since the train is the Cinque Terre's lifeline, shops, hotels, and restaurants often post the current schedule, and many also hand out copies of it (one also comes with the Cinque Terre Park Card). I find the printed schedules a bit confusing since certain departures listed are for only weekdays, only Sundays, and so on (check the key carefully). Monitors in the train stations (described next) are your best source of actual, current departure information. Sometimes it's easiest to do as the locals do: Stop by the station and check the screens to see the next departure time; if it's a ways off, enjoy an ice-cream cone, a bit more shopping, or some beach time.

Important: Any train stopping at Vernazza, Corniglia, or Manarola is going to all the towns. Trains from Monterosso, Riomaggiore, or La Spezia sometimes skip lesser stations, so confirm that the train will stop at the town you need.

At the Platform: Convenient TV monitors posted at several places in each station clearly show what times the next trains in each direction are leaving (and, if they're late—*in ritardo*—how many minutes late they are expected to be). On the monitors, northbound trains are marked for *Genova, Levanto,* or *Sestri Levante;* southbound trains are marked for *La Spezia* or *Sarzana.* (Most northbound trains that stop at all Cinque Terre towns will list Sestri Levante as the *destinazione.*) To be sure you get on the right train, it helps to know your train's number and final destination.

Assuming you're on vacation, accept the unpredictability of Cinque Terre trains—they're often late, unless you are, too, in which case they're on time. Relax while you wait—buy a cup of coffee at a station bar. Scout the platform you need in advance, and then, when the train comes, casually walk over and hop on. This is especially easy in Monterosso, with its fine café-with-a-view on track #1 (direction: Milano/Genova), and in Vernazza, where you can hang out at the Blue Marlin Bar with a prepaid drink and dash when the train pulls in.

Getting Off: Know your stop. As the train leaves the town just before your destination, go to the door and get ready to slip out before the mobs flood in (making it impossible to get off). A word to the wise for novice tourists, who often miss their stop: The stations are small and the trains are long, so (especially in Vernazza) you might have to get off deep in a tunnel. Also, the doors don't open automatically—you may have to open the handle of the door yourself (twist the black handle, or lift up the red one). If a door isn't working, go quickly to the next car to leave.

Alternative: Remember that boats connect the towns about as frequently as the trains, though at different times (see next); if you're in a rush, take whichever form of transport is leaving first.

By Boat

From Easter through October, a daily boat service connects Monterosso, Vernazza, Manarola, Riomaggiore, and Portovenere.

Though they can be very crowded, these boats provide a scenic way to get from town to town and survey where you just hiked. And boats offer the only efficient way to visit the nearby resort of Portovenere (see next chapter); the alternative is a tedious train-bus connection via La Spezia.

In peaceful weather, the boats can be more reliable than the trains, but if seas are rough, they don't run at all. Because the boats nose in and tourists have to gingerly disembark onto little more than a plank, even a small chop can cancel some or all of the stops.

I see the tour boats as a syringe, injecting each town with a boost of euros. The towns are addicted, and they shoot up hourly through the summer. (Between 10:00 and 15:00—especially on weekends—masses of gawkers unload from boats, tour buses, and cruise ships, inundating the villages and changing the feel of the region.)

Boats depart Monterosso about hourly (10:30-17:00), stopping at the Cinque Terre towns (except at Corniglia) and ending up an hour later in Portovenere. (Portovenere-Monterosso boats run 8:50-17:00.) The ticket price depends on the length of the boat ride (ranging from €2 for a very short ride between towns, to €3.50 between towns farther apart, up to €11 for a five-town, one-way ticket with stops; a five-town all-day pass costs €15). Round-trip tickets are slightly cheaper than two one-way trips. You can buy tickets at little stands at each town's harbor (tel. 0187-732-987 and 0187-818-440). Another all-day boat pass for €25 extends to Portovenere and includes a 40-minute scenic ride around three small islands (2/day). Boats are not covered by the standard Cinque Terre Park Card, but the planned Blu card may include them (ask). Boat schedules are posted at docks, harbor bars, Cinque Terre park offices, and hotels (www.navigazionegolfodeipoeti.it).

By Shuttle Bus

Green shuttle buses (which locals call *pulmino*) connect each Cinque Terre town with its distant parking lot and various points in the hills (for example, a shuttle runs from Corniglia's train station to its hilltop town center). Note that these shuttle buses do not connect the towns with each other. Most rides cost €1.50 one-way (buy tickets from driver; buses are also covered by the Cinque Terre Park Card). You can ask about bus schedules at TIs and park info offices, or note the times posted at bus stops, but be aware that shuttle service is quite unreliable. Confirm the details carefully before planning your day around the bus. As you board, it's always smart to tell the driver where you want to go. Departures often coordinate with train arrival times. Some (but not all) departures from Vernazza, Manarola, and Riomaggiore go beyond the parking lots and high into the hills. To soak in the scenery, you can pay €2.50 for a round-trip ride and just cruise both ways (30-45 minutes round-trip).

Hiking the Cinque Terre

All five towns are connected by good trails, marked with red-and-white paint, white arrows, and some signs. *Sentiero* means trail.

The region has several numbered *sentieri*, but most visitors stick to the main coastal trail that connects the villages—that's trail #2 (described in the next section). For extra credit, get local advice for detours to dramatic hilltop sanctuaries. I've outlined my favorite non-#2 hike, from Manarola over Volastra to Corniglia, later.

Trail Closures: Trails can be closed in bad weather or because of landslides. (In fact, in summer of 2013, all four segments of the popular coastal trail were closed for one reason or another.) Before planning your hiking day, carefully confirm whether any of trail segments are closed. Official closures are noted on the national park website (www.parconazionale5terre.it), and the national park information desks in each town's train station post a list. However, sometimes a trail is "officially" closed—meaning that its ticket desk is closed—but still able to be hiked (at your own risk). It's worth asking locals or fellow hikers for the latest on which trails are passable and which aren't.

Hiking Conditions: Other than the wide, easy Riomaggiore-Manarola segment, the coastal trail is generally narrow, steep, rocky, and comes with lots of challenging steps. I get many emails from readers who say the trail was tougher than they'd expected. The rocks and metal grates can be slippery in the rain (I'd avoid the very steep Monterosso-Vernazza stretch if it's wet). And if you venture up on those rocky cliffs without sun protection or water, you deserve the sunburn and dehydration that will result. While the trail is challenging, it's perfectly doable for any fit hiker...and worth the sweat.

When to Go: The coastal trail can be very crowded (and very hot) at midday. The best times to hike are early in the day (before the crowds and heat hit) and late in the day. Before setting out for an evening hike, find out what time the sun sets, and leave yourself plenty of time to arrive at your destination before then; after dark, there's no lighting on the trails.

Navigation: Maps aren't necessary for the basic coastal hikes described here. But for the expanded version of this hike (12 hours, from Portovenere to Levanto) and more serious hikes in the high country, pick up a good hiking map (about €5, sold everywhere). The *Cinque Terre Walking Guide* (by a German publisher, but sold locally in an English-language edition for about €15) is worth seeking out for anyone planning a serious hike. The national park's free, official Cinque Terre ViTour Hiking Guide smartphone app provides trail information (including updates on which trails are open or closed); it is currently available only in Italian, but they hope to launch an English version soon.

Give a Hoot: To leave the park cleaner than you found it, bring a plastic bag *(sacchetto di plastica)* and pick up a little trail trash along the way. It would be great if American visitors—who get so much joy out of this region—were known for this good deed.

Weather: As in many communities whose livelihoods are tied to the sea, locals have names for the different types of winds: *Scirocco* is a cloudy, warm, southeasterly wind from North Africa; it carries sand from the Sahara, which makes a mess as it scatters over the land. The *scirocco* causes a condition called *macaia*—sticky, heavy, wet, still, and overcast weather believed to put everyone in a rotten mood. Conversely, the *tramontana* is a cool, clear, refreshing, northerly breeze that comes "across the mountains," bringing sunny weather and calm seas. The *libeccio* wind, from the southwest (and named for Libya), means "sun but big waves." The *maestrale* is a stiff westerly that generally comes with sunny weather (and isn't as intense as France's notorious mistral). And *grecale* is a strong, cold, northeasterly wind from Russia that produces chilly drizzle and sometimes snow in the mountains.

The Coastal Trail

You'll experience the area's best by hiking from one end of the coastal trail to the other—that means Riomaggiore to Monterosso, or vice versa. (Be aware that segments of this trail can close without warning—see "Trail Closures," earlier.) The entire seven-mile coastal hike (on trail #2) can be done in about four hours, but allow five for dawdling. Germans (with their task-oriented *Alpenstock* walking sticks) are notorious for marching too fast through the region. Take it slow...smell the cactus flowers and herbs, notice the scurrying lizards, listen to birds singing in the olive groves, and enjoy vistas on all sides.

If you're hiking the full five-town route, consider these factors: The trail between Riomaggiore (#1) and Manarola (#2) is easiest.

The hike between Manarola and Corniglia (#3) has minor hills (for a much steeper, more scenic alternative, consider detouring higher up, via Volastra—described later). The trail from Corniglia to Vernazza (#4) is demanding, and the path from Vernazza to Monterosso (#5) is the most challenging. The hike I describe goes from town #1 (Riomaggiore) to #5 (Monterosso), but some hikers prefer the opposite direction. Starting in Monterosso allows you to tackle the toughest section (with lots and lots of steep, narrow stairs) while you're fresh—and to enjoy some of the region's most dramatic scenery as you approach Vernazza. You can also mix-and-match, splitting up the hike over several days, depending on your home base and itinerary, the weather, and the time of day. Remember that hikers need to pay a fee to enter the trails (see "Cinque Terre Park Cards," earlier).

Riomaggiore-Manarola (20 minutes): The popular, easy **Via dell'Amore** (as it's called) was washed out by a landslide in 2013;

they hope to reopen it in early 2014—inquire locally. If it's open, facing the front of the train station in Riomaggiore (#1), go up the stairs to the right, following signs for *Via dell'Amore*. The photo-worthy promenade—wide enough for baby strollers—winds along the coast to Manarola (#2). While there's no beach along the trail, stairs lead down to sunbathing rocks. A long tunnel and mega-nets protect hikers from mean-spirited falling rocks. A recommended wine bar—Bar & Vini A Piè de Mà—is located at the Riomaggiore trailhead and offers light meals, awesome town views, and clever boat storage under the train tracks. There's a picnic zone with a water fountain, shade, and a seagull that must have been human in a previous life hanging out just above the Manarola station (WC at Manarola station). If the trail is closed, you can connect these towns by train...or, far more scenically, with a €2 boat trip.

Manarola-Corniglia (45 minutes): The walk from Manarola (#2) to Corniglia (#3) is a little longer, more rugged, and steeper than the Via dell'Amore. It's also less romantic. To avoid the last stretch (switchback stairs leading up to the hill-capping town of Corniglia), end your hike at Corniglia's train station and catch the shuttle bus to the town center (2/hour, €1.50, free with Cinque Terre Park Card, usually timed to meet the trains).

Corniglia-Vernazza (1.5 hours): The hike from Corniglia (#3) to Vernazza (#4)—the wildest and greenest section of the coast—is very rewarding but very hilly (going the other direction, from Vernazza to Corniglia, is steeper). From the Corniglia station

CINQUE TERRE

Via dell'Amore

The Cinque Terre towns were extremely isolated until the last century. Villagers rarely married anyone from outside their

town. After the blasting of a second train line in the 1920s, a trail was made between the first two towns, Riomaggiore and Manarola. The gunpowder warehouses built on each end, safely away from the townspeople, house cute little bars today.

Happy with the trail, the villagers asked that it be improved as a permanent connection between neighbors. But persistent landslides kept the trail closed more often than it was open. After World War II, the trail was reopened and became established as a lovers' meeting point for boys and girls from the two towns. (After one extended closure in 1949, the trail was reopened for a Christmas marriage.) A journalist who noticed all the amorous graffiti along the path coined the trail's now-established name, Via dell'Amore: "Pathway of Love."

This new lane changed the social dynamics between the two villages, and made life much more fun and interesting for courting couples. Today, many tourists are put off by the cluttered graffiti that lines the trail. But it's all part of the history of the Cinque Terre's little lovers' lane.

You'll see padlocks locked to wires, cables, and fences. Closing a padlock with your lover at a lovey-dovey spot—often a bridge—is a common ritual in Italy (it was re-popularized by a teen novel a few years ago). In case you're so inclined, the hardware store next to Bar Centrale in Riomaggiore sells these locks. (You'll notice many of the locks come with the park logo.)

Major construction work—including the addition in 1994 of tunnels—has made the trail safer. Notice how the brick-lined arcades match the train tunnel below. Rock climbers from the north ("Dolomite spiders") were imported to help with the treacherous construction work. As you hike, look up and notice the massive steel netting bolted to the cliffside. Look down at the boulders that fell before the nets were added, and up at the boulders that have been caught...and be thankful for those Dolomite spiders.

Continuing the romance theme, benches along the way are named for lovers from Greek mythology. The many agave plants sport carved love notes—etched by amorous couples who likely don't know that the plant, which flowers once and then dies, is named for a tragic Greek story.

and beach, zigzag up to the town (via the steep stairs, the longer road, or the shuttle bus). Keep going through vineyards toward Vernazza, and after about ten minutes, you'll see Guvano beach far beneath you (once the region's nude beach). The scenic trail leads through a virtually deserted village, past picnic tables, through lots of fragrant and flowery vegetation, into Vernazza. If you need a break before reaching Vernazza, stop by Franco's Ristorante and Bar la Torre; it has a small menu but big views.

Vernazza-Monterosso (1.5 hours): The trail from Vernazza (#4) to Monterosso (#5) is a scenic up-and-down-a-lot trek and the most challenging of the bunch. Trails are narrow, steep, and crumbly, with a lot of steps (some readers report "very dangerous"), but easy to follow. Locals frown on camping at the picnic tables located midway. The views just out of Vernazza, looking back at the town, are spectacular. From there you'll gradually ascend, passing some scenic waterfalls populated by croaking frogs. As you approach Monterosso, you'll descend steeply—on very tall, knee-testing stairs—through vineyards, eventually following a rivulet to the sea. The last stretch into Monterosso is along a pleasant, paved pathway clinging to the cliff. You'll pop out right at Monterosso's refreshing old town beach.

Longer Hikes

While the national park charges admission for the coastal trails, they also maintain a free, far more extensive network of trails higher in the hills. Shuttle buses make the going easier, connecting coastal villages and distant trailheads. For pointers, ask at a TI or park office—or anyone who's helpful (the Manarola-based Cinque Terre Trekking is a good resource).

Manarola-Volastra-Corniglia via the High Road (2.5 hours): One option—particularly if the Manarola-Corniglia trail is closed (and, if you're into serious hikes, even if it isn't)—is the hike from Manarola up to the village of Volastra, then north through high-altitude vineyard terraces, and steeply down through a forest to Corniglia (about six miles total). You can shave the two steepest miles off this route by taking the shuttle bus from Manarola up to Volastra (€1.50 or free with Cinque Terre Park Card, schedule at park office, about hourly, 15 minutes). If you prefer to hike, you have two options for getting from Manarola to Volastra. The national park's official route (trail #6) cuts up through the valley, with less scenery. Locals have cleared a more scenic alternate route that begins with the vineyard hike on my self-guided walk for Manarola. Partway along this walk, when you reach the wooden religious scenes scampering up the hillside, take a sharp right and walk uphill, following the signs for *Volastra panoramica (Corniglia)*. While steeper than the official route, this trail follows the ridge at the top of the vineyard, providing wonderful sea views.

By shuttle bus or by one of the trails, you'll reach Volastra. This tiny village, perched between Manarola and Corniglia, hosts lots of Germans and Italians in the summer. (Just below its town center, in the hamlet of Groppo, is the Cinque Terre Cooperative Winery.) When you're ready to head for Corniglia, make your way to the village church (where the shuttle bus drops off) and look for *Corniglia* signs. You'll circle around to the front door of the church; directly across the piazza, find the trailhead (marked by an iron cross) for trail #6d to Case Pianca. Here begins one of the finest hikes in the region, tight-roping along narrow trails tucked between vineyard terraces, with spectacular bird's-eye views over the entire Cinque Terre. You'll cut up and down the terraces a bit—just keep following the red-and-white markings and arrows. After passing a little village (and following the signs through someone's seaview backyard), the trail enters a forest and begins its sharp, rocky descent into Corniglia. (To skip the descent, you could turn around and hike back through the vineyards to Volastra and return by shuttle bus to Manarola.) High above Corniglia, you'll reach a fork, where you turn left to proceed downhill on trail #7a to Corniglia.

Other Longer Hikes: If parts of the main coastal trail are closed and you're here for some serious hiking, get tips from locals on alternative trails. Popular options include **Vernazza to Reggio** (straight up the ridge, along Stations of the Cross, to the Sanctuary of Madonna; about an hour one-way, but easier if you take the shuttle bus from Vernazza); **Monterosso to Levanto** (about 3.5 hours one-way, moderately strenuous); and **Riomaggiore to Portovenere** (about 5 hours one-way; a challenging trek best for serious hikers). Be sure to get specific pointers before you set out.

Swimming, Kayaking, and Biking

Every town in the Cinque Terre has a beach or a rocky place to swim. Monterosso has the biggest and sandiest beach, with umbrellas and beach-use fees (but it's free where there are no umbrellas). Vernazza's main beach is tiny—better for sunning than swimming; the new, flood-created beach there is bigger. Manarola and Riomaggiore have the worst beaches (no sand), but Manarola offers the best deep-water swimming.

Wear your walking shoes and pack your swim gear. Several of the beaches have showers (no shampoo, please). Underwater sightseeing is full of fish—goggles are sold in local shops. Sea urchins can be a problem if you walk on the rocks, and sometimes jellyfish wash up on the pebbles, so water shoes (or at least flip-flops) are essential.

You can rent kayaks or boats in Riomaggiore and Monterosso.

(For details, see individual town listings in this chapter.) Some readers say kayaking can be dangerous—the kayaks tip easily, training is not provided, and lifejackets are not required.

Sleeping in the Cinque Terre

If you think too many people have my book, avoid Vernazza. You get fewer crowds and better value for your money in other towns. Monterosso is a good choice for sun-worshipping softies, those who prefer the ease of a real hotel, and the younger crowd (more nightlife). Hermits, anarchists, wine lovers, and mountain goats like Corniglia. Sophisticated Italians and Germans choose charming but not overrun Manarola, which has a good range of (relatively) professional-feeling small accommodations, but limited dining options. Riomaggiore—bigger than Vernazza and less resorty than Monterosso—has the cheapest beds, but hoteliers there tend to be a bit flakier.

While the Cinque Terre is too rugged for the mobs that ravage the Spanish and French coasts, it's popular with Italians, Germans, and in-the-know Americans. Hotels charge more and are packed on holidays (including Easter); in May, June, and September; and on Fridays and Saturdays all summer. (With global warming, sweltering August is no longer considered peak season on this stretch of the Riviera.) While you can find doubles for €65 or €70 most of the season, you'll pay extra (around €80) in May and June. The prices I've listed are the maximum for April through October. For a terrace or view, you might pay an extra €20 or more. Apartments for four can be economical for families—figure around €120.

It's smart to reserve your room in advance in May, June, July, and September, and on weekends and holidays. At other times,

you can land a double room on any day just by arriving in town (ideally by noon) and asking around at bars and restaurants, or simply by approaching locals on the street. Many travelers enjoy the opportunity to shop around a bit and get the best price by bargaining. Private rooms—called *affitta camere*—are no longer an intimate stay with a family. They are generally comfortable apartments (often with small kitchens), where you get the key and come and go as you like, rarely seeing your landlord. Many landowners rent the buildings by the year to local managers, who then attempt to make a profit by filling them night after night with tourists. While air-conditioning is essential in the summer elsewhere in Italy, in the breezy Cinque Terre you can generally manage fine without it.

For the best value, visit several private rooms and snare the best. Going direct cuts out the middleman and softens prices. Staying more than one night gives you bargaining leverage. Plan on paying cash. Private rooms are generally bigger and more comfortable than those offered by pensions and have the same privacy as a hotel room.

If you want the security of a reservation, make it at a hotel long in advance (smaller places generally don't take reservations very far ahead). If you do reserve, do it by email, and be sure to honor your reservation (or, if you must cancel, do it as early as possible). Since people renting rooms usually don't take deposits, they lose money if you don't show up. The more formal places tend to have strict cancellation policies.

Most of the private rooms don't include breakfast, so I've suggested alternatives in each town. The basic, very Italian choice is simply to drop by a neighborhood bar to buy a coffee and *cornetto* or a croissant. Some pricier places "include breakfast," but this usually consists of a few paltry items (yogurt, instant coffee, stale croissant) in a mini-fridge in your room.

Eating in the Cinque Terre

Hanging out at a seaview restaurant while sampling local specialties could become one of your favorite memories.

The key staple here is anchovies (*acciughe;* ah-CHOO-gay)— ideally served the day they're caught. There's nothing cool about being an anchovy virgin. If you've always hated anchovies (the harsh, cured-in-salt American kind), try them fresh here. They can be prepared a variety of ways: marinated, salted, butterflied and deep-fried (sometimes with a delicious garlic/vinegar sauce called *giada*), and so on. *Tegame alla vernazzana* is the most typical main course in Vernazza: a layered, casserole-like dish of whole anchovies, potatoes, tomatoes, white wine, oil, and herbs.

While antipasto means cheese and salami in Tuscany, here you'll get *antipasti frutti di mare* (sometimes called simply *antipasti misti*), a plate of mixed "fruits of the sea" and a fine way to start a meal. Many restaurants are particularly proud of their *antipasti frutti di mare*—it's how they show off. For two diners, splitting one of these and a pasta dish can be plenty.

This region is the birthplace of pesto. Basil, which loves the temperate Ligurian climate, is ground with cheese (half parmigiano cow cheese and half pecorino sheep cheese), garlic, olive oil, and pine nuts, and then poured over pasta. Try it on spaghetti or, better yet, on *trenette* (the long, flat Ligurian noodle ruffled on one side) or *trofie* (short, dense twists made of flour with a bit of potato), both designed specifically for pesto to cling to. Many also like pesto lasagna, always made with white sauce, never red. If you become addicted, small jars of pesto are sold in the local grocery stores and gift shops. If it's refrigerated, it's fresh; this is what you want if you're eating it today. For taking home, get the jar-on-a-shelf pesto.

Pansotti are ravioli with ricotta and a mixture of greens, often served with a walnut sauce...delightful and filling.

Focaccia, the tasty pillowy bread, also originates here in Liguria. Locals say the best focaccia is made between the Cinque Terre and Genoa. It's simply flatbread with olive oil and salt. The baker roughs up the dough with finger holes, then bakes it. Focaccia comes plain or with onions, sage, or olive bits, and is a local favorite for a snack on the beach. Bakeries sell it in rounds or slices by weight (a portion is about 100 grams, or *un etto*).

Farinata, a humble fried-bread snack, is made from chickpea meal, water, oil, and pepper and baked on a copper tray in a wood-burning stove. *Farinata* is sold at pizza and focaccia places.

The *vino delle Cinque Terre*, while not one of Italy's top wines, flows cheap and easy throughout the region. It's white—great with seafood. For a sweet dessert wine, the *Sciacchetrà* wine is worth the splurge (€4 per small glass, often served with a cookie). You could order the fun dessert *torta della nonna* ("grandmother's cake") and dunk chunks of it into your glass. Aged *Sciacchetrà* is dry and costly (up to €12/glass). While 10 kilos of grapes yield 7 liters of local wine, *Sciacchetrà* is made from near-raisins, and 10 kilos of grapes make only 1.5 liters of *Sciacchetrà*. The word means "push and pull"—push in lots of grapes, pull out the best wine. If your room is up a lot of steps, be warned: *Sciacchetrà* is 18 percent alcohol, while regular wine is only 11 percent.

In the cool, calm evening, sit on Vernazza's breakwater with a glass of wine and watch the phosphorescence in the waves.

Nightlife in the Cinque Terre

While the Cinque Terre is certainly not noted for bumping beach-town nightlife like nearby Viareggio, you'll find some sort of travel-tale-telling hub in Monterosso, Vernazza, and Riomaggiore (Manarola and Corniglia are sleepy). Monterosso (where bars can stay open until 2:00 in the morning) has a lively scene, especially in the summertime—but no *discoteca*...yet. In Vernazza, the nightlife centers in the bars on the waterfront piazza, which is the small-town-style place to "see and be seen." A town law requires all bars to shut by midnight. In Riomaggiore, Bar Centrale is the, well, central place for cocktails and meeting fellow travelers. (For details, see the "Nightlife" sections for these three villages.) Wherever your night adventures take you, have fun, but please remember that residents live upstairs.

CINQUE TERRE

Helpful Hints for the Cinque Terre

Tourist and Park Information: Each town has a well-staffed park information office, which generally serves as an all-purpose town TI as well (listed throughout this chapter).

Money: Banks and ATMs are plentiful throughout the region.

Baggage Storage: You can store bags at La Spezia's train station (€3/12 hours, 8:00-22:00) and at the Wash and Dry Lavarapido in Monterosso (€5/day).

Services: Every train station has a handy, free public WC. Otherwise, pop into a bar or restaurant.

Taxi: Cinqueterre Taxi covers all five towns (mobile 334-776-1946 or 347-652-0837, www.cinqueterretaxi.com).

Local Guides: Andrea Bordigoni is both knowledgeable and a delight (€110/half-day, €175/day, mobile 393-133-9409, bordigo@inwind.it). Other local guides are **Marco Brizzi** (mobile 328-694-2847, www.hi-ke.com, marco_brizzi@yahoo.it) and **Paola Tommarchi** (paolatomma@alice.it).

Booking Agency: Miriana at **Cinque Terre Riviera** books rooms in the Cinque Terre towns, Portovenere, and La Spezia for a 10 percent markup over the list price (can also arrange transportation, cooking classes, and weddings; Via Roma 24 in Vernazza or Via Picedi 18 in La Spezia; tel. 0187-520-702, mobile 340-794-7358, www.cinqueterreriviera.com, info@ cinqueterreriviera.com, English spoken).

Tours and Activities: ArbaSPàa, which has an office in Manarola, can arrange Cinque Terre experiences that might be tricky to do on your own, such as wine-tasting at a vineyard, cooking classes (6-person minimum), or a fishing trip with local sailors (see website for options and book in advance, tel. 0187-920-785, www.arbaspaa.com; their Explora shop in Manarola, at Via Discovolo 204, is closed Tue).

Riomaggiore (Town #1)

The most substantial non-resort town of the group, Riomaggiore is a disappointment from the train station. But just walk through the tunnel next to the train tracks, and you'll discover a more real, laid-back, and workaday town than its touristy neighbors. The main drag through town, while traffic-free, feels more urban than "village," and surrounding the harbor is a fascinating tangle of pastel homes leaning on each other like drunken sailors.

Orientation to Riomaggiore

Tourist Information

The TI is in the train station at the ticket desk (daily 8:00-18:00, tel. 0187-920-633). If the TI in the station is crowded, buy your hiking pass at the Cinque Terre park shop/information office next door, facing the mural (daily 7:00-19:00, shorter hours off-season, tel. 0187-760-515). For informal information sources, try Ivo and Alberto, who run Bar Centrale (see "Nightlife in Riomaggiore," later) or Amy and Francesco, who run Riomaggiore Reservations (see "Sleeping in Riomaggiore," later).

Arrival in Riomaggiore

By Train: Riomaggiore's train station is separated from the town center by a steep hill (which you can summit for fine views by following my self-guided walk). The easiest way to get into town is to take the pedestrian tunnel that begins by the big mural (and parallels the rail tunnel). You'll exit at the bottom of Via Colombo; most recommended hotels are a short hike up this steep artery. If you're staying near the top of town and want to skip the walk, you can catch the shuttle bus (described next) at the bottom of Via Colombo and ride it partway up.

By Car: Day-trippers are not allowed to drive into Riomaggiore; you'll have to park at the lot above town (€1.50/hour), then walk or ride the shuttle bus downtown (€1.50 one-way, €2.50 round-trip, free with Cinque Terre Park Card, 1-2/hour but almost comically erratic, main stop at the fork of Via Colombo and Via Malborghetto, or flag it down as it passes). If you're staying overnight, seek the advice of your hotelier, who may have a line on their own parking or can fill you in on all the logistics of public parking

CINQUE TERRE

(which tend to change frequently). Riomaggiore allows overnighters to drive into the town center long enough to drop off your bags, but only during designated times (likely Mon-Fri 6:00-10:00 & 14:00-16:00, Sat 6:00-10:00 only, not on Sun—but confirm with your hotelier).

Helpful Hints

Internet Access: The **park shop/information office** has four Internet terminals upstairs, plus Wi-Fi (€1.50/20 minutes, hours listed earlier, under "Tourist Information"). **La Zorza Café** and **Bar Centrale** both offer free Wi-Fi with the purchase of a drink (see "Nightlife in Riomaggiore," later).

Laundry: A self-service launderette is on the main street (€3.50/ wash, €3.50/dry, €1/soap, daily in summer 8:30-20:00, shorter hours off-season, run by Edi's Rooms next door, Via Colombo 111).

Self-Guided Walk

Welcome to Riomaggiore

Here's a partly uphill but fairly easy loop trip that takes the long way around from the station into town. You'll enjoy some fine views before strolling down the main street to the harbor. (If you're arriving for an overnight stay and packing heavy bags, drop them off at your hotel before starting this walk.)

• *Start at the train station. (If you arrive by boat, cross beneath the tracks and take a left, then hike through the tunnel along the tracks to reach the station.) You'll come to some...*

Colorful Murals: These murals, with subjects modeled after real-life Riomaggiorians, glorify the nameless workers who con-

structed the nearly 300 million cubic feet of dry-stone walls (made without mortar) that run throughout the Cinque Terre. These walls give the region its characteristic *muri a secco* terracing for vineyards and olive groves. The murals, created by Argentinean artist Silvio Benedetto, are explained well in English.

Looking left, notice the stairs climbing up just past the station building. These lead to the trail to Manarola, also known as the **Via dell'Amore**.

• *The fastest way into town is to take the pedestrian tunnel (which parallels the tracks from near the murals) straight to the bottom of Via Colombo, just above the marina. But I'd rather take the scenic route, up and over the hill. Before starting, you can check to see if the elevator near the entrance to the tunnel is running (but I doubt it). More likely, you'll have to hoof it: Facing the mural, turn left, then go right up the wide street just before the station café. Watch for the stairs leading through the garden on your right to the upper switchback, then, once on high ground, hook back toward the sea. Soon you'll pass the concrete tower marking the top of the elevator we saw earlier, and a bit farther, a fine viewpoint.*

Top o' the Town: Here you're treated to spectacular sea views. Hook left around the bluff; once you round the bend, ignore the steps marked *Marina Seacoast* (which lead to the harbor) and continue another five minutes along level ground to the church. You'll pass under the city hall, with murals celebrating the heroic grape-pickers and fishermen of the region (also by Silvio Benedetto).

• *Before reaching the church, pause to enjoy the...*

Town View: The major river of this region once ran through this valley, as implied by the name Riomaggiore (local dialect for "river" and "major"). As in the other Cinque Terre towns, the river ravine is now paved over, and the romantic arched bridges that once connected the two sides have been replaced by a practical modern road.

Notice the lack of ugly aerial antennae. In the 1980s, every residence got cable. Now, the TV tower on the hilltop behind the church steeple brings the modern world into each home. The church was rebuilt in 1870, but was first established in 1340. It's dedicated to St. John the Baptist, the patron saint of Genoa, the maritime republic that once dominated the region.

• *Continue straight past the church and along the narrow lane, watching on the right for wide stairs leading down to Riomaggiore's main street...*

Via Colombo: As in the other Cinque Terre towns, the main street of Riomaggiore covers its *rio maggiore*, which carved the canyon now filled by the town's pastel high-rises. Across from where you came down the stairs, notice the handy public WCs. Then start downhill. First you'll pass (on the right, at #62) a good pizzeria/*focacceria,* facing the Co-op grocery store across the street (at #55). Farther down on the left is the town butcher (*marcelleria,* #103). The big covered terrace on the right belongs to Bar Centrale, the town's most popular hangout for international visitors (at #144; see "Nightlife in Riomaggiore," later). Just after the terrace sits a forlorn row of recycling containers, with careful instructions that are ignored by locals and tourists alike.

As you round the bend to the left, notice the old-timey pharmacy just above (on the right). On your left, at #199, peek into the Il Pescato Cucinato shop, where Laura fries up her husband Eduardo's fresh catch; grab a paper cone of deep-fried seafood as a snack. Where the road bends sharply right, notice the bench on your left (just before La Zorza Café)—the hangout for the town's old-timers, who keep a running commentary on the steady flow of people. Straight ahead, you can already see where this street will dead-end. The last shop on the left, Alimentari Franca (at #251), is a well-stocked grocery where you can gather the makings for a perfect picnic out on the harbor or along the Via dell'Amore.

Where Via Colombo dead-ends, look right to see the tunnel leading back to the station (and the Via dell'Amore to Manarola, and eventually to the other Cinque Terre towns). Look left to see two sets of stairs. The "up" stairs take you to a park-like square built over the train tracks, which provides the children of the town a bit of level land on which to kick their soccer balls. The murals above celebrate the great-grandparents of these very children—the salt-of-the-earth locals who earned a humble living before the age of tourism.

• *The "down" stairs take you to the...*

Marina: This most picturesque corner of Riomaggiore features a tight cluster of buildings huddling nervously around a postage-stamp square and vest-pocket harbor. Because Riomaggiore lacks the naturally protected harbor of Vernazza, when bad weather is expected, local fishermen pull their boats up to the safety of the little square. This is quite an operation, so it's a team effort—the signal goes out, and anyone with a boat of their own helps move the whole fleet. Sometimes the fishermen are busy beaching their boats even on a bright, sunny day—an indication that they know something you don't know.

A couple of recommended restaurants—with high prices and memorable seating—look down over the action. Head past them and up the walkway along the left side of the harbor, and enjoy the views of the town's colorful pastel buildings, with the craggy coastline of the Cinque Terre just beyond. Below you, the break-water curves out to sea, providing a bit of protection for the harbor. These rocks are popular with sunbathers by day and romantics and photographers at sunset.

For a peek at Riomaggiore's beach, continue around the bluff on this trail toward the Punta di Montenero, the cape that defines the southern end of the Cinque Terre. As you walk you'll pass the rugged boat landing and eventually run into Riomaggiore's uncomfortably rocky but still inviting beach *(spiaggia)*. Ponder how Europeans manage to look relaxed when lounging on football-sized "pebbles."

Sights in Riomaggiore

Beach

Riomaggiore's rugged and tiny "beach" is rocky, but it's clean and peaceful (to find it, see the end of my self-guided walk, above).

CINQUE TERRE

To Manarola

♥ Via dell'Amore ♥

Cliffs

Ligurian Sea

PARK OFFICE
KIOSK
TRAIN
STATION

WALK
BEGINS

MURALS

CINQUE
TERRE INFO

VIA PECUNIA

VIA SIGNORINI

VIA

PEDESTRIAN
TUNNEL

VIA SANT'ANTONIO

PUNTA

B

Cliffs

Harbor

BOAT DOCK

VIA SAN GIACOMO

BREAKWATER

BOAT
TICKETS

1. Riomaggiore Reservations (Office), Il Pescato Cucinato, Giammi Caffè & Co-op Grocery
2. Edi's Rooms & Launderette
3. L'Ancora Rooms
4. Alla Marina Rooms; Enoteca & Ristorante Dau Cila
5. La Dolce Vita Rooms
6. Il BoMa Rooms
7. Locanda del Sole
8. Locanda dalla Compagnia
9. Camere Patrizia
10. La Lanterna Ristorante
11. Trattoria la Grotta & Il Grottino Ristorante
12. Bar Centrale & Gelateria
13. Pizzeria/Focacceria
14. Te La Do Io La Merenda Snack Bar
15. Alimentari Franca
16. Bar & Vini A Piè de Mà
17. La Zorza Café
18. Co-op Grocery

There's a shower here in the summer, and another closer to town by the boat landing—where many enjoy sunning on and jumping from the rocks.

Kayaks and Water Sports

The town has a diving center (scuba, snorkeling, kayaks; office down the stairs and under the tracks on Via San Giacomo, daily May-Sept 9:00-18:00, open in good weather only—likely weekends only in shoulder season, tel. 0187-920-011, www.5terrediving.it).

Hikes

It's possible to hike from here all the way to Portovenere (about 5 strenuous hours). Some easier alternatives are also available. A trail rises scenically from Riomaggiore to the 14th-century Madonna di Montenero sanctuary, high above the town (45 minutes, take the main road inland until you see signs, or ride the green shuttle bus 12 minutes from the town center to the sanctuary trail, then walk uphill another 10 minutes; great picnic spot up top). The cliff-hanging Torre Guardiola trail, a steep 20-minute climb from the beach up to old WWII bunkers and a hilltop botanical pathway, has been closed indefinitely because of a rock slide.

Nightlife in Riomaggiore

Bar Centrale, run by sociable Ivo, Alberto, and the gang, offers "nightlife" any time of day—making it a good stop for Italian breakfast and music. Ivo, who lived in San Francisco, fills his bar with San Franciscan rock and a fun-loving vibe. During the day, this is a shaded place to relax with other travelers; it feels a little like the village's living room. At night, it offers the younger set the liveliest action (and best mojitos) in town (daily 7:30-1:00 in the morning, closed Mon in winter, 30 minutes of free Wi-Fi with drink, in the town center at Via Colombo 144, tel. 0187-920-208). They plan to open a restaurant nearby, serving Italian classics as well as comfort food for homesick Americans. The good *gelateria* next door has the same name but different owners.

Enoteca & Ristorante Dau Cila, a cool little hideaway with a mellow jazz-and-Brazilian-lounge ambience down at the miniscule harbor, is a counterpoint to wild Bar Centrale. It's cool for cocktails and open nightly until 24:00 (snacks and meals, fine wine by the glass; see "Eating in Riomaggiore," later).

Bar & Vini A Piè de Mà, at the beginning of Via dell'Amore, has piles of charm, €6 cocktails, frequent music, and stays open until midnight June through September (see "Eating in Riomaggiore," later).

La Zorza Café is a hip, youthful alternative to the other bars in town. The music is thumping, and the cocktails come with a spread of little snacks (€6 cocktails, daily until 1:00 in the morning, free Wi-Fi with drink, tel. 0187-920-036, fun-loving Elenia).

The marvelous **Via dell'Amore** trail (described earlier), lit only with subtle ground lighting so that you can see the stars, welcomes romantics after dark. The trail is free after 19:30.

Sleeping in Riomaggiore

Riomaggiore has arranged its private-room rental system somewhat better than its neighbors. Several agencies—with relatively predictable office hours, English-speaking staff, and email addresses—line up within a few yards of each other on the main drag. Each manages a corral of local rooms for rent—but be aware that quality and specific amenities can vary wildly, so get a complete picture of the room before you commit. These offices sometimes close unexpectedly, so it's smart to settle up the day before you leave in case they're closed when you need to depart. Expect lots of stairs.

Room-Booking Services
Given the relatively lousy value of Riomaggiore's hotels (see next section), I'd contact one of these services first. Keep in mind that very few of these rooms include breakfast.

$$ Riomaggiore Reservations, run with care and smooth communication by American expat Amy and her Italian husband Francesco, offers 12 rooms and 15 apartments (Db-€60-90 depending on view, Db suite with top view-€120, discount if you pay cash, reception open daily 9:00-13:00 & 14:00-17:00 in season, some rooms have air-con, free Wi-Fi at office; parking-€10/day at the top of town—reserve in advance; Via Colombo 181, tel.

Sleep Code

(€1 = about $1.30, country code: 39)
S = Single, **D** = Double/Twin, **T** = Triple, **Q** = Quad, **b** = bathroom, **s** = shower only. Unless otherwise noted, credit cards are accepted, English is spoken, and breakfast is included (except in Vernazza). Many towns in Italy levy a hotel tax of €2 per person, per night, which must be paid in cash (not included in the rates I've quoted).

To help you sort easily through these listings, I've divided the accommodations into three categories based on the price for a standard double room with bath:

$$$ Higher Priced—Most rooms €100 or more.
　$$ Moderately Priced—Most rooms between €50-100.
　　$ Lower Priced—Most rooms €50 or less.

Prices can change without notice; verify the hotel's current rates online or by email. For the best prices, always book direct.

0187-760-575, www.riomaggiorereservations.com, info@riomaggiorereservations.com).

$$ Edi's Rooms manages 20 rooms and apartments. You pay extra for views (Db-€70-100 depending on size/view/location, apartment Qb-€140-180, reserve with credit card, office open daily in summer 8:30-20:00, in winter 10:30-12:30 & 14:30-18:00, some rooms involve climbing a lot of steps—ask, some rooms have air-con and/or free Wi-Fi, reception at Via Colombo 111, tel. 0187-760-842, tel. 0187-920-325, www.appartamenticinqueterre.net, edi-vesigna@iol.it). They also rent three hotelesque but pricey rooms of their own, called **L'Ancora** (Db-€120, air-con, free Wi-Fi, www.lancoracinqueterre.com).

Private Rooms

Another option is to book direct with someone who rents just a few rooms of their own, cutting out the middleman. Here are some options.

$$$ Alla Marina is Riomaggiore's most worthwhile splurge, with three rooms and an apartment (all but one with sea views) at the top of one of the very tall, steep, skinny buildings that rise up from the harbor. The furnishings are a stylish combination of modern and nautical, and friendly Sandro takes pride in running a tight ship (non-view Db-€100, view Db-€120, view Tb-€135, view Qb-€180, includes breakfast in room, air-con, free minibar, free Wi-Fi, parking-€10/day; Via San Giacomo 61—ask Sandro about the easier back-door entrance; mobile 328-013-4077, www.allamarina.com, info@allamarina.com).

$$ La Dolce Vita offers five nice, good-value rooms on the main drag, plus two apartments elsewhere in town (Db-€65-80, open daily 9:30-19:30—if they're closed, they're full; Via Colombo 167, tel. 0187-762-283, mobile 329-099-2741, agonatal@libero.it, helpful Giacomo and Simone).

$$ Il BoMa—named for the owners, American Maddy and her Italian husband Bombetta—has three pricey but well-appointed rooms right along the main drag (Db-€90, includes breakfast in room, one has private bathroom down the hall and fans, the others have air-con, free Wi-Fi, up three flights at Via Colombo 99, tel. 0187-920-395, mobile 320-0748826, www.ilboma.com, info@ilboma.it).

Hotels

Perhaps sensing that they have little "hotel" competition, these options generally offer less value than the room-booking services and private rooms. Breakfast is included in their rates.

$$$ Locanda del Sole has seven modern, basic, and overpriced rooms with a shared and peaceful terrace. Located at the utilitarian top end of town, it's a five-minute walk downhill to the center. Easy (and free with this book) parking makes it especially appealing to drivers (Db-€130, air-con, free Wi-Fi in common areas, Via Santuario 114, tel. 0187-920-773, mobile 340-983-0090, www.locandadelsole.net, info@locandadelsole.net, Enrico).

$$ Locanda dalla Compagnia, loosely run by Allessandro, rents five rooms at the top of town, just 300 yards below the parking lot and the little church. All rooms—decent but rather dim—are on the same tranquil ground floor and share a lounge (Db-€80, air-con, mini-fridge, no views, free Wi-Fi, reception closes at 19:00, Via del Santuario 232, tel. 0187-760-050, www.dallacompa.com, lacomp@libero.it). Allessandro also manages nine apartments scattered around town, which cost the same as his hotel rooms (but don't include breakfast).

Backpacker Dorms

$ Riomaggiore Reservations (also listed earlier) runs a mini-hostel in a fine communal apartment with eight beds in two rooms, a cool living room, a terrace, and a kitchen in a good, quiet location. They also have a four-bed unit with no terrace. Take care of this little treasure so it survives (€25/bed, reception open 9:00-13:00 & 14:00-17:00 in season, free Wi-Fi, Via Colombo 181, tel. 0187-760-575, www.riomaggiorereservations.com, info@riomaggiorereservations.com).

$ Camere Patrizia, a suitable last resort, rents cheap doubles (Db-€60, €70 on weekends) and dorm bunk beds (€25/person) from its reception at Via Colombo 25, but books only through www.hostelworld.com or to drop-ins (reception open daily 10:30-20:00, free Wi-Fi in office, mobile 328-309-3727).

Eating in Riomaggiore

On the Harbor

Harborfront dining comes with slightly higher prices but glorious views.

Enoteca & Ristorante Dau Cila (pronounced "dow CHEE-lah") is decked out like a black-and-white movie set in a centuries-old boat shed with extra tables outside on a rustic deck over dinghies. Try their antipasto specialty of several seafood appetizers and listen to the waves lapping at the harbor below (€13-15 pastas, €15-18 *secondi;* for lunch, they also have a simpler menu—€9-12 salads and *bruschette;* daily 12:00-24:00, closed Feb, Via San Giacomo 65, tel. 0187-760-032, Luca).

La Lanterna, with a gray-and-white interior and a few appealing harborview tables outside, is wedged into a niche in the Marina, overlooking the harbor under the tracks. Chef Massimo serves traditional plates, loves anchovies, and bakes fresh bread daily (€10-11 pastas, €12-18 *secondi,* no cover, daily 12:00-22:00, Via San Giacomo 10, tel. 0187-920-589).

On the Main Street, Via Colombo

Trattoria la Grotta, right in the town center (with no view), serves reliably good food with a passion for anchovies and mussels. You'll enjoy friendly service surrounded by historical photos and wonderful stonework in a dramatic, dressy, cave-like setting. Venessa is warm and helpful, while her mother, Isa, is busy cooking (€11-14 pastas, €11-15 *secondi,* 5 percent discount if you pay cash, daily 12:00-14:30 & 17:30-22:30, closed Wed in winter, Via Colombo 247, tel. 0187-920-187). Next door and run by the same family, **Il Grottino Ristorante** is slightly more upscale, with a similar approach and decor and a somewhat different menu (same hours, tel. 0187-920-938). I'd survey both to see which specials look good.

Bar Centrale, the popular bar and expat hangout, plans to begin serving American comfort food; for a break from pizza and pasta, drop by to scope out their menu (see "Nightlife in Riomaggiore," earlier).

Light Meals: Various handy carry-out eateries along the main drag offer good lunches or snacks on the go. At the top of town, the nameless **pizzeria/focacceria** at #62 is a reliable standby (€3 slices). For deep-fried seafood in a paper cone, two places face each

CINQUE TERRE

other across the main street near the bottom of town; of these, I prefer **Il Pescato Cucinato,** where Eduardo fishes and his wife Laura fries (€5-7, chalkboard out front explains what's fresh, daily 11:20-20:30, Via Colombo 199, mobile 339-262-4815). **Te La Do Io La Merenda** has a counter piled with an assortment of munchies, including pizza and focaccia sandwiches (€3 light meals, daily 10:00-20:00, Via Colombo 161, mobile 340-400-3256).

Picnics: Groceries and delis lining Via Colombo sell food to go for a picnic at the harbor or beach. Look for the two *Co-Op* grocery store signs for the best prices. The handy **Alimentari Franca,** at the very bottom of the main street (conveniently located right by the train-station tunnel and stairs down to the marina/beach) has a more appealing selection and good service (Thu-Tue 8:00-12:45 & 15:30-19:30, closed Wed, Via Colombo 251).

Breakfast: While hotels include breakfast, many private rooms don't, and those that do often simply leave some basic continental breakfast fixings in your room's mini-fridge. For a good croissant-and-espresso fix, drop by **Bar Centrale** (which may expand its menu in the future). If you need eggs, consider **Giammi Caffè,** with outdoor tables on the main drag (€5 egg dishes, €13 big breakfast, daily 7:00-24:00, Via Colombo 189, mobile 331-608-3512).

Near the Train Station and Via dell'Amore

Bar & Vini A Piè de Mà, at the trailhead on the Manarola end of town, is good for a scenic light bite or quiet drink at night. The downstairs bar, with all of the great outdoor seating, is self-service: Head into the bar to place your order, then bring it out to your preferred perch (€8-12 dishes, €4 *panini*, daily 10:00-20:00, June-Sept until 24:00, free Wi-Fi—look for password on chalkboard, tel. 0187-921-037). Enjoying a meal at a table on its dramatically situated terrace provides an indelible Cinque Terre memory. In the summer they open a restaurant with table service upstairs—but I prefer the cheaper, simpler terrace.

Manarola (Town #2)

Mellow Manarola fills a ravine, bookended by its wild little harbor to the west and a diminutive hilltop church square inland to the east. Manarola is exceptional for being unexceptional: While Vernazza is prettier, Monterosso glitzier, Riomaggiore bigger, and Corniglia more rustic, each of those towns is also sorely lacking in other regards. Manarola hits a fine balance, giving it the "just right" combination of Cinque Terre qualities. Perhaps that's why it's a favorite among savvy Europeans seeking a relatively untrampled home base. The touristy zone squeezed between the cement-encased train tracks and the harbor can be stressfully congested, but head just a few steps uphill and you can breathe again. The higher you go, the less crowded it gets, culminating in the essentially tourist-free residential zone that clings to the ridge.

Manarola, whose hillsides are blanketed with vineyards, also provides the easiest access to the Cinque Terre's remarkable dry-stone terraces. The trail ringing the town's cemetery peninsula, adjacent to the main harbor, provides some of the most easily accessible and most strikingly beautiful town views anywhere in the region (best light late in the day). For a look at all the facets of this delightful town, follow my gentle self-guided stroll from the church, through the vineyards, and down to the harborside park.

Orientation to Manarola

Tourist Information: As in other Cinque Terre towns, Manarola's train station has a TI/national park information office (likely daily 7:00-19:00, shorter hours off-season).

Getting Around: The national park's green **shuttle bus** runs from near the post office (halfway up Manarola's main street), stopping first at the parking lots above town, and then going all the way up to Volastra (€1.50 one-way, €2.50 round-trip, buy ticket on board, free with Cinque Terre Park Card, about hourly, just flag it down). Volastra is a great jumping-off point for a scenic hike through vineyards and forests to Corniglia (more challenging—and rewarding—than the official coastal trail).

To get to the **dock** and the boats that connect Manarola with the other Cinque Terre towns, find the steps to the left of the harbor view—they lead down to the ticket kiosk. Continue around the left side of the cliff (as you're facing the water) to catch the boats.

Wi-Fi, Laundry, and Hiking Gear and Tips: Cinque Terre Trekking, near the top of the main street (halfway up to the church), fills its cramped little shop with hiking gear; they also sell hiking maps (with free advice), offer pay Wi-Fi, and have a few self-service laundry machines (€10/load wash and dry, daily 9:00-13:00 & 14:00-20:00, shorter hours off-season, Via Discovolo 136, tel. 0187-920-715).

Arrival in Manarola

On Foot: Walking in from Riomaggiore on the Via dell'Amore, you'll pop out at Manarola's train station (see next).

By Train: Like Riomaggiore, Manarola is attached to its station by a 200-yard-long tunnel (lined with interesting photos). During WWII air raids, these tunnels provided refuge and a safe place for rattled villagers to sleep. Walking through the tunnel, you'll reach Manarola's elevated square (created by covering the tracks). To reach the busy harbor (with touristy restaurants, the boat dock, and the start of my self-guided walk), cross the piazza, then go down the other side. To reach the town, hilltop church, and vineyard strolls, turn right.

By Car: Unless you're sleeping here, you're not allowed to drive into Manarola. Park your car in one of the two lots just before town (€1.50/hour), then walk down the road to the church; from there, the street twists down to the main piazza, train-station tunnel (to reach the trailhead for the Via dell'Amore to Riomaggiore), and harbor (the start of my self-guided walk). It's an easy downhill walk into town, or you can wait for the national park's shuttle bus (described earlier). If you're sleeping here, ask your hotelier for parking advice: You'll likely be allowed to drive into town to drop off your bags—but only during certain hours (likely Mon-Fri 6:00-10:00 & 14:00-16:00, Sat 6:00-10:00 only, not on Sun—confirm locally)—before heading back to the lot to park.

Self-Guided Walk

Welcome to Manarola

From the harbor, this 30-minute circular walk shows you the town and surrounding vineyards and ends at a fantastic viewpoint, perfect for a picnic.

• *Start down at the waterfront. Belly up to the wooden banister overlooking the rocky harbor, between the two restaurants.*

The Harbor: Manarola is tiny and picturesque, a tumble of buildings bunny-hopping down its ravine to the fun-loving waterfront. The breakwater—which attempts to make this jagged harbor a bit less dangerous—was built just over a decade ago. Notice how the I-beam crane launches the boats (which must be pulled ashore when bad weather is expected to avoid being smashed or swept away).

Facing the water, look to the right, at the hillside Punta Bonfiglio cemetery and park. The trail running around the base of the point—where this walk ends—offers magnificent views back on this part of town.

The town's swimming hole is just below you. Manarola has no sand, but offers the best deep-water swimming in the area. The first "beach" has a shower, ladder, and wonderful rocks. The second has tougher access and no shower, but feels more remote and pristine (follow the paved path toward Corniglia, just around the point). For many, the tricky access makes this "beach" dangerous.

• *Hiking inland up the town's main drag—comparison-shopping at the touristy restaurants—you'll climb a steep ramp to reach Manarola's "new" square, which covers the train tracks.*

Piazza Capellini: Built in 2004, this square is an all-around great idea, giving the town a safe, fun zone for kids. Locals living near the tracks also enjoy a little less train noise. Check out the mosaic in the middle of the square, which depicts the varieties of local fish in colorful enamel. The recommended Ristorante di Aristide has an inviting terrace right out on the square.

• *Go down the stairs at the upper end of the square. On your right, notice the tunnel that leads to Manarola's train station (and the trailhead for the Via dell'Amore to Riomaggiore). But for now, head up...*

Via Discovolo: Manarola's sleepy main street twists up through town, lined by modest shops and filled with pooped hikers. Just before the road bends sharply right, watch (on the right) for a waterwheel. This recalls the origin of the town's name—local dialect for "big wheel" (one of many possible derivations). Mills like this once powered the local olive oil industry. As you continue up (all the way to the church), you'll still hear the rushing waters of Manarola's stream. Like the streams in Riomaggiore, Monterosso, and Vernazza, Manarola's rivulet was covered over by a modern sewage system after World War II. Before that time, romantic bridges arched over its ravine. You can peek below the concrete street in several places to see the stream surging below your feet.

Across the street from the waterwheel and a bit farther up, notice the **Cinque Terre Trekking** shop (on your left), which outfits hikers with both information and gear (boots, clothes, walking sticks, and more).

• *Keep switchbacking up until you come to the square at the...*

Top of Manarola: The square is faced by a church, an oratory—now a religious and community meeting place—and a bell tower, which served as a watchtower when pirates raided the town (the cupola was added once the attacks ceased). Behind the church is Manarola's well-run youth hostel, originally the church's schoolhouse. To the right of the oratory, a stepped lane leads to Manarola's sizable tourist-free residential zone.

Check out the **church.** According to the white marble plaque in its facade, the Parish Church of St. Lawrence (San Lorenzo)

CINQUE TERRE

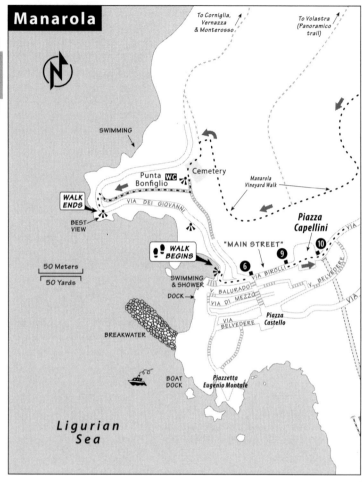

dates from "MCCCXXXVIII" (1338). Step inside to see two altar-piece paintings from the unnamed Master of the Cinque Terre, the only painter of any note from this region (left wall and above main altar). While the style is Gothic, the work dates from the late 15th century, long after Florence had entered the Renaissance. Note the humble painted stone ceiling, which replaced the wooden original in the 1800s. It features Lawrence, patron saint of the Cinque Terre, with his grill, the symbol of his martyrdom (he was roasted on it).

• *With the bell tower on your left, head about 20 yards down the main street below the church and find a wooden railing. It marks the start of a delightful stroll around the high side of town, and back to the seafront. This is the beginning of the...*

To Volastra (Official trail)

To Volastra (car, shuttle bus)

VIA LITORANEA

SP-370

TUNNEL

To ⑧

Manarola Vineyard Walk Entrance

VIA DISCOVOLO

BELL TOWER

POST

SAN LORENZO CHURCH

ORATORY

DISCOVOLO

ROLLANDI

RESIDENTIAL ZONE

Piazza Papa Innocenzo IV

PEDESTRIAN TUNNEL

TRAIN STATION

Via dell'Amore ♥ Trail

To Riomaggiore

① La Torretta Rooms
② Aria di Mare Rooms
③ B&B Da Baranin
④ Ostello 5-Terre
⑤ Albergo Ca' d'Andrean
⑥ Marina Piccola Rooms & Restaurant
⑦ Affitta Camere da Paulin
⑧ To Hotel il Saraceno
⑨ Trattoria il Porticciolo
⑩ Ristorante di Aristide
⑪ Via Discovolo Eateries
⑫ Trattoria dal Billy
⑬ Cinque Terre Trekking
⑭ Shuttle Bus to Parking Lot & Volastra

Manarola Vineyard Walk: Don't miss this experience. Simply follow the wooden railing, enjoying lemon groves and wild red valerian (used for insomnia since the days of the Romans). Along the path, which is primarily flat, you'll get a close-up look at the region's famous dry-stone walls and finely crafted vineyards (with dried-heather thatches to protect the grapes from the southwest winds). Smell the rosemary. Study the structure of the town, and pick out the scant remains of an old fort. Notice the S-shape of the main road—once a riverbed—that flows through town. The town's roofs are traditionally made of locally quarried slate, rather than tile, and are held down by rocks during windstorms.

Halfway along the lip of the ravine, a path marked *Volastra panoramico (Corniglia)* leads steeply up into the vineyards on the right. This path passes a variety of simple wooden religious scenes, the work of local resident Mario Andreoli. Before his father died, Mario promised him he'd replace the old cross on the family's vineyard. Mario has been adding figures ever since. After recovering from a rare illness, he redoubled his efforts. On religious holidays, everything's lit up: the Nativity, the Last Supper, the Crucifixion, the Resurrection, and more. Some of the scenes are left up year-round. High above, a recent fire burned off the tree cover, revealing ancient terraces that line the terrain like a topographic map. This path also marks the start of the scenic route to Volastra (on the hilltop above), and eventually to Corniglia (a challenging alternative to the standard coastal route).

• *Continue on the level trail around the base of the hill. Soon the harbor comes into view. Keep looping around the hill for even better views of town. Once you're facing the sea (with the cemetery peninsula below you), the trail takes a sharp left and heads down toward the water. When you hit the clifftop fence, the T-intersection gives you a choice: right, to the coastal trail to Corniglia, or left, back to town. Turn left for now. Before descending, watch for the turnoff on the right, detouring into...*

The Cemetery: Ever since Napoleon—who was king of Italy in the early 1800s—decreed that cemeteries were health risks, Cinque Terre's burial spots have been located outside the towns. The result: The dearly departed generally get first-class sea views. Each cemetery—with evocative yellowed photos and finely carved Carrara marble memorial reliefs—is worth a visit. (The basic structure for all of them is the same, but Manarola's is the most easily accessible.)

In cemeteries like these, there's a hierarchy of four places to park your mortal remains: a graveyard, a spacious death condo *(loculo)*, a mini bone-niche *(ossario)*, or the communal ossuary. Because of the tight space, a time limit is assigned to the first three options (although many older tombs are grandfathered in). Bones go into the ossuary in the middle of the chapel floor after about a generation. Traditionally, locals make weekly visits to loved ones here, often bringing flowers. The rolling stepladder makes access to top-floor *loculi* easy.

• *The Manarola cemetery is on...*

Punta Bonfiglio: This point offers some of the most commanding views of the entire region. To find the best vantage point, take the stairs just below the cemetery (through the green gate), then walk farther out toward the water through a park (playground, drinking water, WC, and picnic benches). Your Manarola finale is the bench at the tip of the point. Pause and take in the view. The easiest way back to town is to take the stairs at the end of the point, which join the main walking path—offering more spectacular town views on its way back to the harbor, where we started.

Sleeping in Manarola

Manarola's accommodations seem a bit more professional than the other towns (except, perhaps, Monterosso). Like the others, it has plenty of private rooms; ask in bars and restaurants.

In the Residential Zone Above the Church

This area is about a 10-minute uphill hike from the train station—just huff up the main drag to the church. All of these are within a five-minute walk from there.

$$$ La Torretta is a trendy, upscale 13-room place that caters to a demanding clientele. Probably the most elegant retreat in the region, it's a peaceful refuge with all the comforts for those happy to pay, including a communal hot tub with a view. Enjoy a complimentary snack and glass of prosecco on arrival, free wine-tastings during your stay, breakfast in your room, and a free minibar. Each chic room is distinct and described on their website (smaller Db-€145, regular Db-€190, Db suite-€250-400, 10 percent discount when you pay cash, book several months in advance as it's justifiably popular, closed mid-Nov-mid-March, pay Wi-Fi, on Piazza della Chiesa beside the bell tower at Vico Volto 20, tel. 0187-920-327, www.torrettas.com, torretta@cdh.it).

$$$ B&B Da Baranin, with six good rooms and four apartments, is overpriced but nicely located just above the church (Db-€110, bigger "superior" Db-€130, includes breakfast; apartments: Db-€120, Tb-€140, Qb-€160, no breakfast; air-con, free Wi-Fi, Via Aldo Rollandi 29, tel. 0187-920-595, www.baranin.com, info@baranin.com).

$$ Aria di Mare Rooms rents four sunny rooms and an apartment 20 yards beyond Trattoria dal Billy at the very top of town. If you don't mind staying in a mostly residential zone high above the tourists, this is a great value. Three rooms have spacious terraces with knockout views and lounge chairs. Maurizio speaks a little English, while Mamma Franca communicates with lots of Italian and toothy smiles (Db-€85, Db apartment-€90, these prices promised through 2014, includes basic breakfast in room, air-con, free Wi-Fi, upstairs on the left at Via Aldo Rollandi 137, tel. 0187-920-367, mobile 349-058-4155, www.ariadimare.info, info@ariadimare.info, ask at Billy's if no one's home).

$ Ostello 5-Terre, Manarola's modern and pleasant hostel, occupies the former parochial school above the church square and offers 48 beds in four- to six-bed rooms. Nicola runs a calm and peaceful place—it's not a party hostel—and quiet is greatly appreciated. They rent dorm rooms as doubles. Reserve well in advance (dorm beds-€24, Db-€65, Qb-€100; 20 percent less mid-Oct-Easter, not co-ed except for couples and families, no membership necessary, open to all ages, optional €2-5 breakfast and bargain dinners, office closed 13:00-16:00—except maybe in summer, rooms closed 10:00-13:00, check-in until 22:00, elevator, free Wi-Fi, lockers, book exchange, Via B. Riccobaldi 21, tel. 0187-920-039, www.hostel5terre.com, info@hostel5terre.com).

On the Main Street

These options line up along the main street, between the harbor and the church. While in a less atmospheric area than the ones near the church, they're closer to the station—and therefore a bit handier for those packing heavy.

$$$ Albergo Ca' d'Andrean, run by Simone, is quiet, comfortable, and modern. It has 10 big, sunny, air-conditioned rooms and a cool garden oasis complete with lemon trees. If you don't mind stairs, try requesting one of their top-floor rooms, with great views from their terraces (Sb-€75, Db-€105, breakfast-€6, free Wi-Fi, up the hill at Via Discovolo 101, tel. 0187-920-040, www.cadandrean.it, info@cadandrean.it).

$$$ Marina Piccola offers 13 bright, slick rooms on the water (some with sea views), but the rooms are an afterthought to their busy tourist-trap restaurant. They're planning to renovate their rooms, so prices may increase (Db-€120, air-con, free Wi-Fi, Via Birolli 120, tel. 0187-762-065, www.hotelmarinapiccola.com, info@hotelmarinapiccola.com).

$$ At **Affitta Camere da Paulin,** charming Donatella and Eraldo (the town's retired policeman) rent three very nice, well-equipped rooms with a large and inviting common living room, plus three apartments. It's in a modern setting a few minutes' walk uphill from the train tracks (Db-€100, view apartment Db-€140, Qb-€180, usually requires a 3-night minimum stay, air-con, free Wi-Fi, Via Discovolo 126, tel. 0187-920-706, mobile 334-389-4764, www.dapaulin.it, prenotazioni@dapaulin.it).

High Above Manarola, in Volastra

$$ Hotel il Saraceno, with seven spacious, modern, functional rooms, is a deal for drivers. Located above Manarola in the tiny town of Volastra (chock-full of vacationing Germans and Italians in summer), it's serene, clean, and right by the shuttle bus to Manarola (Db-€100, buffet breakfast, free Wi-Fi, free parking, località AVA, tel. 0187-760-081, www.thesaraceno.com, hotel@thesaraceno.com, friendly Antonella).

Eating in Manarola

Restaurant options are limited in Manarola. I've listed these in order, from lowest to highest, in terms of quality and elevation.

The vast majority of the town's restaurants (all of them decidedly touristy) are concentrated in the tight zone between Piazza Capellini and the harbor. While these are mostly interchangeable, the Scorza family works hard at **Trattoria il Porticciolo** (€7-10 pastas, €9-18 *secondi*, Thu-Tue 7:30-23:30, closed Wed, Via Birolli 92, tel. 0187-920-083). At the harborfront itself, **Marina Piccola** is famous for great views, lousy service, and price-gouging naive tourists.

Ristorante di Aristide, right on Piazza Capellini, offers trendy atmosphere and a pleasant, less claustrophobic outdoor setting, with a view of budding soccer stars rather than harborfront glitz (€8-12 pastas, €10-19 *secondi*). Down the stairs, at the bottom of the main street, their simpler **café** has indoor and streetside seating and a simpler menu (€5-7 pizzas, sandwiches, and salads; both open Tue-Sun 8:00-22:30, closed Mon, Via Discovolo 290, tel. 0187-920-000).

Via Discovolo, the main street climbing up through town from Piazza Capellini to the church, is lined with simpler places, including a popular *gelateria* and some small grocery stores where you can browse for a picnic.

Up at the very top of town, in the residential zone above the church, dining options are sparse, but the one place that's here is a good one: **Trattoria dal Billy** offers both good food and impressive views over the valley. With Edoardo and Enrico's black pasta with seafood and squid ink, green pasta with artichokes, mixed seafood starters, and homemade desserts, many find it worth the climb. Dinner reservations are a must (€8-12 pastas, €13-20 *secondi*, generally daily 8:00-15:00 & 19:00-23:30, closed Thu, Via Aldo Rollandi 122, tel. 0187-920-628).

Corniglia (Town #3)

This tiny, sleepy town—the only one of the five not on the water—owns a mellow main square. According to a (likely fanciful) local legend, the town was originally settled by a Roman farmer who named it for his mother, Cornelia (how Corniglia is pronounced). The town and its ancient residents produced a wine so famous that—some say—vases found at Pompeii touted its virtues. Regardless of the veracity of the legends, wine remains Corniglia's lifeblood today. Follow the pungent smell of ripe grapes into an alley cellar and get a local to let you dip a straw into a keg.

Remote and less visited than the other Cinque Terre towns, Corniglia has fewer tourists, cooler temperatures, a few restaurants, a windy overlook on its promontory, and plenty of private rooms for rent (ask at any bar or shop, no cheaper than other towns). Because of the long, steep hike between the town and its train station (give yourself at least 15 minutes to rush down and catch your train, or use the shuttle bus) and Corniglia's lack of a boat dock, it's a less convenient home base for town-hopping. If you think of the Cinque Terre as the Beatles, Corniglia is Ringo.

Orientation to Corniglia

Tourist Information

As in all Cinque Terre towns, a TI/park information office is at the train station (likely daily 7:00-19:00, shorter hours off-season).

Arrival in Corniglia

By Train: From the station, filling a gloomy ravine far below town, a footpath zigzags up 385 steps (and nearly that many switchbacks) to the town. If you'd rather not walk, take the green shuttle bus—generally timed to meet arriving trains—which connects the station with Corniglia's main square, the start of my self-guided walk (€1.50 one-way, €2.50 round-trip, buy ticket as you board, free with Cinque Terre Park Card, 1-2/hour).

By Car: Only residents can park on the main road between the recommended Villa Cecio and the point where the steep switchback staircase meets the road. Beyond that area, parking is €1.50/ hour. Fortunately, all parking areas are within an easy and fairly level walk of the town center.

Self-Guided Walk

Welcome to Corniglia

We'll explore this tiny town—population 240—and end at a scenic viewpoint. This walk might take up to 30 minutes...but only if you let yourself browse and lick a gelato cone.

• *Begin near the bus stop, located at a...*

Town Square: The gateway to this community is "Ciappà" square, with an ATM, phone booth, old wine press, and bus stop (shuttle buses timed to coordinate with train schedules). The Cinque Terre's designation as a national park sparked a revitaliza-

Corniglia

To Vernazza

200 Meters
200 Yards

CINQUE TERRE

LOC. CANALE
VIA SERRA
LOC. CHIOSO
VIA ALLA STAZIONE
VIA FIESCHI
VIA ALLA MARINA
VIA
385 STEPS
VIA LARDARINA

❸
❻
❷ ❽ ❹
❶ ❺

Harbor

"CIAPPÀ"
SQUARE &
BUS STOP

To Manarola
Ⓑ ⓘ

TRAIN STATION

SANTA MARIA BELVEDERE

LARGO TARAGIO, ORATORY & ❼

Ligurian Sea

SWIMMING

❶ Pan e Vin Bar
   (Ricci Rooms Check-In)
❷ Il Carugio Rooms & Butiega Shop
❸ Villa Cecio Rooms
❹ Corniglia Hostel
❺ Osteria Mananan &
   Enoteca il Pirun
❻ La Posada Ristorante
❼ La Lanterna Restaurant
❽ Gelateria

tion of the town. Corniglia's young generation is more likely now to stay put, rather than migrate into big cities the way locals did in the past.

• *Look for the arrow pointing to the* centro. *Stroll the spine of Corniglia, Via Fieschi. In the fall, the smell of grapes (on their way to becoming wine) wafts from busy cellars. Along this main street, you'll see...*

Corniglia's Enticing Shops: On the right as you enter Via Fieschi, a pair of neighboring, fiercely competitive *gelaterias* jockey for your business. Both display my book, but my favorite is the second place, **Alberto's Gelateria** (at #74). Before ordering, get a free taste of Alberto's *miele di Corniglia,* made from local honey. His lemon slush *(granita)* takes pucker to new heights.

Farther along, on the left, **Enoteca il Pirùn**—named for a type of oddly shaped old-fashioned wine pitcher designed to aerate the wine and give the alcohol more kick as you squirt it into your mouth—is located in a cool cantina at Via Fieschi 115. Sample some local wines (generally free for small tastes, €3 per glass). If you order wine to drink out of the *pirùn,* Mario will give you a bib. While this is a practical matter (rookies are known to dribble), it also makes a nice souvenir.

In the **Butiega** shop at Via Fieschi 142, Vincenzo sells organic local specialties (daily 8:00-19:30). For picnickers, they offer €4 made-to-order ham-and-cheese sandwiches and a fun *antipasti misti* (priced by the weight). There are good places to picnic farther along on this walk.

• *Following Via Fieschi, you'll end up at the...*

Main Square: On Largo Taragio, tables from two bars and a trattoria spill around a WWI memorial and the town's old well. It once piped in natural spring water from the hillside to locals living without plumbing. What looks like a church is the Oratory of Santa Caterina. (An oratory is a kind of a spiritual clubhouse for a service group doing social work in the name of the Catholic Church.) Up the stairs behind the oratory, you'll find a clearing that local children have made into a soccer field. The stone benches and viewpoint make this a peaceful place for a picnic (less crowded than the end-of-town viewpoint, described next).

• *Opposite the oratory, notice how steps lead steeply down on Via alla Marina to Corniglia's non-beach. It's a five-minute paved climb to sunning rocks, a shower, and a small deck (with a treacherous entry into the water). From the square, continue up Via Fieschi to the...*

End-of-Town Viewpoint: The Santa Maria Belvedere, named for a church that once stood here, marks the scenic end of Corniglia. This is a super picnic spot. From here, look high to the west (right), where the village and sanctuary of San Bernardino straddle a ridge (a good starting point for a hike; accessible by shuttle bus from Monterosso or a long uphill hike from Vernazza). Below is the tortuous harbor, where locals hoist their boats onto the cruel rocks.

Sights in Corniglia

Beaches

This hilltop town has rocky sea access below its train station (toward Manarola). Once a beach, it's all been washed away and offers no services. Look for signs that say *al mare* or *Marina*. A trail leads from the town center steeply down to sunning rocks on the closest thing Corniglia has to a beach (with a shower).

The infamous **Guvano beach** (a bit along the coast toward Vernazza) is now essentially closed down. Guvano was created by an 1893 landslide that cost the village a third of its farmland. Notorious throughout Italy as a nude beach, Guvano was accessed via an unused train tunnel and attracted visitors with an appetite for drug use. Now the tunnel is closed, and the national park wants people to keep their clothes on and forget about Guvano.

Sleeping in Corniglia

(€1 = about $1.30, country code: 39)

Perched high above the sea on a hilltop, Corniglia has plenty of private rooms. To get to the town from the station, catch the shuttle bus or make the 15-minute uphill hike. The town is riddled with humble places that charge too much (generally Db-€65) and have meager business skills and a limited ability to converse with tourists—so it's almost never full.

$$ Cristiana Ricci is an exception to the rule. She communicates well and is reliable, renting four small, clean, and peaceful rooms—two with kitchens and one with a terrace and sweeping view—just inland from the bus stop (Db-€60-70, Tb-€80, Qb-€90, €10/day less when you stay 2 or more nights, free Wi-Fi, check in at the Pan e Vin bar at Via Fieschi 123, mobile 338-937-6547, cri_affittacamere@virgilio.it). Her mom rents two big, modern apartments (€90 for 2-4 people).

$$ Il Carugio has nine modern, sunny rooms right in the center of the village, most with sea views. The communal rooftop terrace offers a commanding view of the coast (Db-€70, Db with seaview balcony-€80, Db apartment-€90 plus €10/extra person, no breakfast, free parking, tel. 0187-812-293, mobile 335-175-7946, www.ilcarugiodicorniglia.com, info@ilcarugiodicorniglia.com, Lidia).

$$ Villa Cecio (pronounced "chay-choe") feels like an abandoned hotel. They offer eight well-worn rooms on the outskirts of town, with saggy beds and little character or warmth. Some rooms have great views, and three have terraces—worth requesting when you check in. All of the rooms share a big rooftop terrace with a grand view (Db-€65 promised in 2014, breakfast-€5, four rooms have air-con, free Wi-Fi, on main road 200 yards toward Vernazza at Via Serra 58, tel. 0187-812-043, mobile 334-350-6637, www.cecio5terre.com, info@cecio5terre.com, Giacinto). They also rent eight similar rooms (Db-€60) in an annex on the square where the bus stops.

$ Corniglia Hostel was formerly the town's schoolhouse. It rents 24 beds in a pastel-yellow building up some steps from the square where the bus stops. The playground in front is often busy with happy kids. Despite its strict and institutional atmosphere, the hostel's prices, central location, and bright and clean rooms ensure its popularity. Its hotelesque double rooms are open to anyone (€24/bed in two 8-bed dorms, four Db-€55—€60 in July-Aug, breakfast-€5, office open 7:00-13:00 & 15:00-1:30 in the morning, dorms closed 10:30-15:00, private rooms closed 13:00-15:00, 1:30 curfew, air-con, lockers, free guest computer and Wi-Fi, self-serve laundry, Via alla Stazione 3, tel. 0187-812-559, www.ostellocorniglia.com, ostellocorniglia@gmail.com).

Eating in Corniglia

Corniglia has few restaurants. The typical array of pizzerias, *focaccerias*, and *alimentari* (grocery stores) line the narrow main drag. For a real meal, consider one of these options.

Osteria Mananan—between the Ciappà bus stop and the main square at Via Fieschi 117—serves what many consider the best food in town in its small, stony, elegant interior (€10 pastas, €10-16 *secondi*, Wed-Mon 12:30-14:30 & 19:30-22:00, closed Tue, no outdoor seating, tel. 0187-821-166).

Enoteca il Pirùn, next door on Via Fieschi, has a small restaurant above the wine bar, where Mario serves typical local dishes (€7-10 pastas, €10-16 *secondi*, €28 fixed-price meal includes homemade wine, daily 12:00-16:00 & 19:30-23:30, tel. 0187-821-075).

La Posada Ristorante offers dinner in a garden under trees, overlooking the Ligurian Sea. To get here, stroll out of town to the top of the stairs that lead down to the station (€8-10 pastas, €10-13 *secondi*, €18 tourist *menù*, daily 12:00-16:00 & 19:00-22:00, tel. 0187-821-174).

The trattoria **La Lanterna,** on the main square, is the most atmospheric, but without particularly charming service (€9-14 pastas, €15-19 *secondi*, daily 12:00-15:00 & 19:30-21:30).

Vernazza (Town #4)

With the closest thing to a natural harbor—overseen by a ruined castle and a stout stone church—Vernazza is the jewel of the

Cinque Terre. Only the occasional noisy slurping up of the train by the mountain reminds you of the modern world.

The action is at the harbor, where you'll find outdoor restaurants, a bar hanging on the edge of the castle, and a breakwater with a promenade, corralled by a natural amphitheater of terraced hills. In the summer, the beach becomes a soccer field, with teams fielded by local bars and restaurants providing late-night entertainment. In the dark, locals fish off the promontory, using glowing bobbers that shine in the waves.

Proud of their Vernazzan heritage, the town's 500 residents like to brag: "Vernazza is locally owned. Portofino has sold out." Fearing the change it would bring, keep-Vernazza-small proponents stopped the construction of a major road into the town and region. Families are tight and go back centuries; several generations live together. In the winter, the population shrinks, as many people return to their more comfortable big-city apartments to spend the money they reaped during the tourist season.

Although Vernazza was hit harder than any other Cinque Terre town by the flood on October 25, 2011 (see sidebar), things are now back to normal. Leisure time is devoted to taking part in the *passeggiata*—strolling lazily together up and down the main street. Sit on a bench and study the passersby doing their *vasche* (laps). Explore the characteristic alleys, called *carugi*. Learn—and live—the phrase *"la vita pigra di Vernazza"* (the lazy life of Vernazza).

Orientation to Vernazza

Tourist Information

There are two information points at the train station, facing each other across the platform between the tracks: One is the gift shop, which can answer basic questions (daily 10:00-13:00 & 14:00-17:00), and the other is the train ticket desk/park office (likely daily 7:00-21:00, shorter hours off-season, tel. 0187-812-533). Public WCs are nearby in the station.

Save Vernazza: Led by a group of American women who married into the community, Save Vernazza brought relief to the town in the immediate aftermath of the 2011 flood and has since morphed into an organization to help preserve and foster healthy tourism. For the latest on their activities, visit www.savevernazza. com.

Arrival in Vernazza

By Train: Vernazza's train station is only about three train cars long, but the trains are much longer—so most of the cars come to a stop in a long, dark tunnel. Get out anyway, and walk through the tunnel to the station. From there the main drag flows through town right to the harbor; my self-guided walk begins just above the station.

By Car: Of the five towns, Vernazza is the most difficult to drive to and park in. The best advice: Park your car in La Spezia and take the train. As of mid-2013, two of the three roads into town were officially closed (the one from Monterosso and the one from the main SP-63 highway above town); the third road, from Corniglia, was open but in rough shape and challenging to drive. Anyone driving from Monterosso to Vernazza should drive up and around the SP-38/SP-1 highway to La Spezia, then follow the road above the other Cinque Terre towns.

CINQUE TERRE

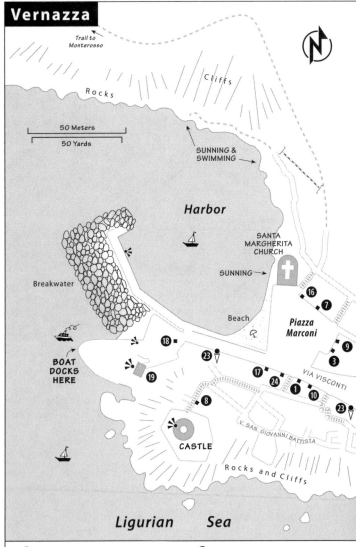

Vernazza

Trail to Monterosso

Cliffs

Rocks

50 Meters
50 Yards

SUNNING & SWIMMING →

Harbor

SANTA MARGHERITA CHURCH

SUNNING →

Breakwater

Beach

Piazza Marconi

BOAT DOCKS HERE

⑱
⑲
⑯
⑦
⑨
③
⑰ ⑭ ① ⑩
⑧
㉓
㉓

VIA VISCONTI

V. SAN GIOVANNI BATTISTA

CASTLE

Rocks and Cliffs

Ligurian Sea

① Trattoria Gianni Reception/Ristorante
② Pensione Sorriso
③ Albergo Barbara Rooms & Francamaria Reception
④ La Perla delle 5Terre Rooms, Tonino Basso Rooms & Il Pirata della Cinque Terre Café & Launderette
⑤ Camere Fontana Vecchia

⑥ Giuliano Basso Rooms
⑦ Martina Callo Rooms, Capitano Rooms Reception & Trattoria del Capitano
⑧ Monica Lercari Rooms
⑨ Nicolina Rooms Reception & Ristorante Pizzeria Vulnetia
⑩ Rosa Vitali Rooms
⑪ Vernazza Rooms Reception & Blue Marlin Bar

Only accommodations with a fixed address or reception (where you check in, then go elsewhere for your room) are listed on this map. For other accommodations, call ahead to arrange a meeting place.

⑫ Rooms Francesca Reception (Enoteca Sciacchetrà) & Ivo's Camere Reception (Pizzeria Fratelli Basso)

⑬ Affitta Camere Alberto Basso Reception & Internet Point

⑭ Eva's Rooms & Trattoria da Sandro

⑮ Rooms Elisabetta (call first)

⑯ Ananasso Bar

⑰ Gambero Rosso Ristorante

⑱ Pizzeria Baia Saracena

⑲ Ristorante Belforte

⑳ Antica Osteria il Baretto

㉑ Ristorante Incadasè da Piva

㉒ Forno Bakery

㉓ Gelaterias (3)

㉔ Burgus Wine Bar

㉕ Franco's Ristorante & Bar la Torre

If you must drive, get precise advice from your hotelier about which roads are open, how to drive in, and where to park (see "Cinque Terre Connections" at the end of this chapter). The visitor parking lot high above town, served by a shuttle bus, washed away in the 2011 flood; a replacement may eventually be built, but it could take years. Yellow lines mark parking spots for residents only.

Helpful Hints

Internet Access: The slick, expensive, six-terminal **Internet Point,** run by Alberto and Isabella, is in the village center (daily June-Oct 9:30-23:00, until 20:00 Nov-May, Wi-Fi, will burn your digital photos to a disc for €5, also sells memory cards). The **Il Pirata delle Cinque Terre** bar (behind/above the train station) and **Blue Marlin Bar** (along the main street) both offer free Wi-Fi with a purchase.

Laundry: The town launderette, at the top of town next to the post office, is completely self-serve (coin-op, €5/wash, €5/dry, includes soap, daily 8:00-22:00, operated by Domenico and Barbara at the fish shop).

Massage: Kate Allen offers a super-relaxing fusion of aromatic/Swedish/holistic massage for €50 per hour in her little studio adjacent to the clinic at the top of Vernazza (tel. 0187-812-537, mobile 333-568-4653, www.vernazzamassage5terre.com).

Best Views: A steep 10-minute hike in either direction from Vernazza gives you a classic village photo op. For the best light, head toward Corniglia in the morning—best views are just before the ticket booth for the national park—and toward Monterosso in the evening—best views are after the ticket booth.

Self-Guided Walk

Welcome to Vernazza

This tour includes Vernazza's characteristic town squares and ends on its scenic breakwater.

• *From the train station, walk uphill along the stream until you hit the small square in front of the Il Pirata delle Cinque Terre bar/café, near the post office. This part of town was particularly damaged during the 2011 flood, but is now being repaired. The stream in this ravine once powered Vernazza's water mill. Shuttle buses run from here to hamlets and sanctuaries in the hills above.*

Walk to the tidy, modern square called...

Fontana Vecchia: Named after a long-gone fountain, this is where older locals remember the river filled with townswomen doing their washing. A lane leads from here up to the cemetery. Imagine the entire village sadly trudging up here during funerals.

(The cemetery is peaceful and evocative at sunset, when the fading light touches each crypt.)

You may see some construction work going on here. Following the 2011 flood, Vernazza attracted worldwide sympathy—including that of prominent architect Richard Rogers (who designed London's Millennium Dome and Lloyd's Building, Wales' National Assembly, and, with frequent collaborator Renzo Piano, Paris' Pompidou Centre). Having enjoyed many relaxing summer vacations in Vernazza, Rogers wanted to give something back. He helped redesign the spine of the town, from here down the main street to the harborfront square (basically the route of this walk). Over the next several years, his plans will help reshape Vernazza. Though Rogers is best known for his dramatically modern designs, his plans for the town are very much in keeping with its traditional soul.

• *Begin your saunter downhill to the harbor. Just before the* Pensione Sorriso *sign, on your right (at #7, with big brown garage doors and a* croce verde Vernazza *sign), you'll see the...*

Ambulance Barn: A group of volunteers is always on call for a dash to the hospital, 40 minutes away in La Spezia. Opposite the barn is a big empty lot. Like many landowners, the owner of Pensione Sorriso had plans to expand, but since the 1980s, the government has said "No." While some landowners are frustrated, the old character of these towns survives. A few steps farther down is the town clinic. The *guarda medica* (emergency doctor—see buzzer) sleeps upstairs.

• *At the corner across from the playground, on a marble plaque in the wall on the left, you'll see a...*

World Wars Monument: This is dedicated to those killed in World Wars I and II. Not a family in Vernazza was spared. Listed on the left are soldiers *morti in combattimento,* who died in World War I; on the right is the WWII section. Some were deported to *Germania;* others—labeled *Part* (for *partigiani,* or partisans, generally communists)—were killed while fighting against Mussolini. Cynics considered partisans less than heroes. After 1943, Hitler called up Italian boys over 15. Rather than die on the front for Hitler, they escaped to the hills and became "resistance fighters" in order to remain free.

The path to Corniglia leaves from here (behind and above the plaque). Behind you is a small square, decorated with a big millstone, once used to grind local olives into oil. There's a good chance you'll see an expat mom here at the village playground with her kids. I've met many American women who fell in love with a local guy, stayed, and are now happily raising families here. (But I've rarely met an American guy who moved in with a local girl.)

From here, Vernazza's tiny river goes underground. Until the

CINQUE TERRE

The Cinque Terre Flood and Recovery

On October 25, 2011, after a very dry summer, a freak rainstorm hit the Cinque Terre. Within four hours, 22 inches of rain fell—a third of an average year's total. Flash floods rushed down the hillsides. Topography allowed the water to quickly drain in Riomaggiore, Manarola, and Corniglia, which were mostly undamaged. But Monterosso and Vernazza were devastated, with much of the two towns buried under 10 feet of mud and left without water, electricity, or phone connections.

The destruction occurred mostly along former ravines, where, historically, streams ran through the towns. In the last century, the ravines were covered with roads, and the streams channeled into underground canals that, over time, were not properly maintained. Like congested arteries, the drainage canals couldn't handle the raging flow. Water pressure caused streets to explode upward. Medieval wells in basements became geysers. Rivers of raging mud carrying rocks, trees, furniture, and even cars and buses rampaged down the main streets, burying the shops and restaurants of old Monterosso and Vernazza. Four locals lost their lives.

The people of the Cinque Terre were taught a tough lesson. It's their beautiful land that brings the tourists. But with the affluence brought by tourism, locals have abandoned their land—leaving vineyards unplanted and centuries-old dry-stone terracing to crumble—for less physically demanding, more profitable work in town. (Grapevines have far-reaching root systems that help combat erosion, and traditional vintners keep their stone terraces in good order.) After a generation of neglect, the unprotected land was washed down into the towns by the violent weather.

Today, you'll find everything in the Cinque Terre back to normal. You may not even realize that in the affected areas of Vernazza and Monterosso, everything is brand-new: stoves, tables, chairs, plates, walls lined with bottles of wine, and so on, all had to be replaced from scratch. Strolling through these towns today, keep in mind everything these people have been through—and appreciate the resilience of the human spirit.

1950s, the river ran openly through the center of town. Old-timers recall the days before the breakwater, when the river cascaded down and the surf sent waves rolling up Vernazza's main drag. Back then, this place was nicknamed "Little Venice" for the series of romantic bridges that arched over the stream, connecting the two sides of the town before the main road was built.

Corralling this stream under the modern street, and forcing it to take a hard right turn here, contributed to the damage caused by the 2011 flood. After the flood, alpine engineers were imported from Switzerland to redesign this drainage system, so any future floods will be less destructive. They also installed nets above the town to protect it from landslides.

The walls under the tracks serve as a sort of community information center. Look for the bulletin board, with a list of local volunteers and when they are on call to drive the ambulance, and info on current events. Across the way, you'll likely see a giant poster with photos of the 2011 flood *(alluvione)* and the shops that it devastated. "The 25th of October" is a day that will live forever in this town's lore. Vernazza is built around one street—basically a lid over the stream in its ravine. On that fateful day, the surrounding hills acted like a funnel, directing flash-flood waters right through the middle of town. As you stroll from here to the harbor, imagine this street buried under 13 feet of mud. Every shop, restaurant, and hotel on the main drag had to be rewired, replumbed, and re-equipped.

The second set of train tracks (nearer the harbor) was recently renovated to lessen the disruptive noise, but locals say it made no difference.

• *Follow the road downhill to...*

Vernazza's "Business Center": Here, you'll pass many locals doing their *vasche* (laps). Next, you'll pass souvenir shops, wine shops, the Blue Marlin Bar (Vernazza's top nightspot), and the tiny Chapel of Santa Marta (the small stone chapel with iron grillwork over the window, on the left), where Mass is celebrated only on special Sundays. Farther down, you'll walk by a *gelateria,* bakery, pharmacy, a grocery, and another *gelateria.* There are plenty of fun and cheap food-to-go options here.

• *On the left, in front of the second* gelateria, *a stone arch was blasted away by the 2011 flood. Scamper through the hole in the rock to reach Vernazza's...*

"New Beach": This is where the town's stream used to hit the sea back in the 1970s. Older locals remember frolicking on a beach here when they were growing up, but the constant, churning surf eventually eroded it all the way back to the cliff. When the 2011 flood hit, it blew out the passageway and deposited landslide material here from the hills above. In the flood's aftermath, Vernazza's main drag and harbor were filled with mud and silt. Workers barged the first batch away, but then—realizing that was an expensive way to remove so much material—decided instead to use the debris to fill in even more of this beach that Mother Nature had violently created. Now Vernazza has a popular beach that feels a world away from the bustle of the main drag. Like other Cinque Terre beaches, this one has no sand, but instead has small pebbles for wading and big rocks for sunning. You'll also find bits of rubble mixed into the pebbles (fragments of roof tiles, perhaps a bit of rusted metal here and there—this is not a barefoot beach). Locals keep unearthing surprising items here. In what could be interpreted as a miracle, a statue of the Madonna—which had been swept off her pedestal by the flood—was recently unearthed here.

Don't get used to this beach. Locals expect that it, like its predecessor, will eventually be washed away.

• *Back on the main drag, continue downhill to the...*

Harbor Square (Piazza Marconi) and Breakwater: Vernazza, with the only natural harbor of the Cinque Terre, was established as the sole place boats could pick up the fine local wine. The two-foot-high square stone at the foot of the stairs by the Burgus Wine Bar (on the left) is marked *Sasso del Sego* (stone of tallow). Workers crushed animal flesh and fat in its basin to make tallow, which drained out of the tiny hole below. The tallow was then used to waterproof boats or wine barrels. Stonework is the soul of the region. Take some time to appreciate the impressive stonework of the restaurant interiors facing the harbor.

On the far side (behind Ristorante Pizzeria Vulnetia), peek into the tiny street with its commotion of arches. Vernazza's most characteristic side streets, called *carugi*, lead up from here. The narrow stairs mark the beginning of the trail that leads up, up, up to the quintessential view of Vernazza—and, eventually, to Monterosso.

Located in front of the harborside church, the tiny piazza—decorated with a river-rock mosaic—is a popular hangout spot. It's where Vernazza's old ladies soak up the last bit of sun, and kids enjoy a patch of level ball field.

Vernazza's harborfront **church** is unusual for its strange entryway, which faces east (altar side), rather than the more typical western orientation. With relative peace and prosperity in the 16th century, the townspeople doubled the church in size, causing it to overtake a little piazza that once faced the west facade. From the square, use the "new" entry and climb the steps, keeping an eye out for the level necessary to keep the church high and dry. Inside, the lighter pillars in the back mark the 16th-century extension. Three historic portable crosses hanging on the walls are carried through town during religious holiday processions. They are replicas of crosses that (locals like to believe) Vernazza ships once carried on crusades to the Holy Land. In 1998, Vernazza's priest was gruesomely and mysteriously murdered. While circumstantial evidence points to fascinating conspiracy theories, no one knows whodunit (or, at least, no one's telling). Today's priest, Don Giovanni, is popular—he stopped the church bells from ringing through the night (light sleepers rejoiced). In the wake of the 2011 flood, he opened up the church as a staging ground for recovery services.

• *Finish your town tour seated out on the breakwater (perhaps with a glass of local white wine or something more interesting from a nearby bar—borrow the glass, they don't mind). Face the town, and see...*

The Harbor: In a moderate storm, you'd be soaked, as waves routinely crash over the *molo* (breakwater, built in 1972). Waves can rearrange the huge rocks—depositing them from the breakwater

onto the piazza and its benches. Freak waves have even washed away tourists squinting excitedly into their cameras. (I've seen it happen.) In 2007, an American woman was swept away and killed by a rogue wave. Enjoy the waterfront piazza—carefully.

The train line (to your left) was constructed in 1874 to tie together a newly united Italy, and linked Turin and Genoa with Rome. A second line (hidden in a tunnel at this point) was built in the 1920s. The yellow building alongside the tracks was Vernazza's first train station. Along the wall behind the tracks, you can see the four bricked-up alcoves where people once waited for trains. Notice the wonderful concrete sunbathing strip (and place for late-night privacy) laid below the tracks along the rocks.

Vernazza's fishing fleet is down to just a few boats (with the net spools). Vernazzans are still more likely to own a boat than a car, and it's said that you stand a better chance of surviving if you mess with a local man's wife than with his boat.

Boats are on buoys, except in winter or when the red storm flag (see the pole at the start of the breakwater) indicates bad seas. At these times, the boats are pulled up onto the square—which is usually reserved for restaurant tables. In the 1970s, tiny Vernazza had one of Italy's top water polo teams, and the harbor was their "pool." Later, when the league required a real pool, Vernazza dropped out.

The Castle (Castello Doria): On the far right, the castle, which is now a grassy park with great views (and nothing but

stones), still guards the town (€1.50 donation, daily 10:00-18:30; from harbor, take stairs by Trattoria Gianni and follow *Ristorante al Castello* signs, tower is a few steps beyond). This was the town's watchtower back in pirate days, and a Nazi lookout in World War II. The castle tower looks new because it was rebuilt after the

British bombed it, chasing out the Germans. The squat tower on the water is great for a glass of wine or a meal. From the breakwater, you could follow the rope to Ristorante Belforte and pop inside, past the actual submarine door. A photo of a major storm showing the entire tower under a wave (not uncommon in the winter) hangs near the bar.

The Town: Before the 12th century, pirates made the coast uninhabitable, so the first Vernazzans lived in the hills above (near the Reggio Sanctuary). The town itself—and its towers, fortified walls, and hillside terracing—are mostly from the 12th through the 15th century, when Vernazza was allied with the Republic of Genoa.

Vernazza has two halves. *Sciuiu* (Vernazzan dialect for "flowery") is the sunny side on the left, and *luvegu* (dank) is the shady side on the right. Houses below the castle were connected by an interior arcade—ideal for fleeing attacks. The "Ligurian pastel" colors are regulated by a commissioner of good taste in the regional government. The square before you is locally famous for some of the area's finest restaurants. The big red central house—on the site where Genoan warships were built in the 12th century—used to be a guardhouse.

In the Middle Ages, there was no beach or square. The water went right up to the buildings, where boats would tie up, Venetian-style. Imagine what Vernazza looked like in those days, when it was the biggest and richest of the Cinque Terre towns. Buildings had a water gate (facing today's square) and a front door on the higher inland side. There was no pastel plaster—just fine stonework (traces of which survive above the Trattoria del Capitano). Apart from the added plaster, the general shape and size of the town has changed little in five centuries. Survey the windows and notice inhabitants quietly gazing back.

While the town has 1,500 residents in summer, only 500 stay here through the winter. Vernazza has accommodations for about 500 tourists.

Above the Town: The small, round tower above the red guardhouse—another part of the city fortifications—reminds us of the town's importance in the Middle Ages. Back then, its key ally Genoa's enemies (i.e., the other maritime republics, especially Pisa) were Vernazza's enemies. Franco's Ristorante and Bar la Torre, just behind the tower, welcomes hikers who are finishing, starting, or simply contemplating the Corniglia-Vernazza hike, with great town views. That tower recalls a time when the entire town was fortified by a stone wall.

Vineyards fill the mountainside beyond the town. Notice the many terraces. Someone—probably after too much of that local wine—calculated that the roughly 3,000 miles of dry-stone walls built to terrace the region's vineyards have the same amount of stonework as the Great Wall of China.

For six centuries, the economy was based on wine and olive oil. Then came the 1980s—and the tourists. Locals turned to tourism to make a living, and stopped tending the land. Many vineyards were abandoned, and the terraces fell into disrepair. But it's the stonework of the terracing in the surrounding hills that helps prevent flooding—a lesson learned in the worst possible way on October 25, 2011.

Although many locals still maintain their tiny plots and proudly serve their family wines, the patchwork of local vineyards is atomized and complex because of inheritance traditions. Historically, families divided their land between their children. Parents wanted each child to get some good land. Because some lots were "kissed by the sun" while others were shady, the lots were split into increasingly tiny and eventually unviable pieces—another reason why many have been abandoned.

A single steel train line winds up the gully behind the tower. It is for the vintner's *trenino*, the tiny service train. Play "Where's *trenino?*" and see if you can find two trains. The vineyards once stretched as high as you can see, but since fewer people sweat in the fields these days, the most distant terraces have gone wild again.

The Church, School, and City Hall: Vernazza's Ligurian Gothic church, built with black stones quarried from Punta Mesco (the distant point behind you), dates from 1318. Note the gray stone that marks the church's 16th-century expansion. The gray-and-red house above the spire is the local elementary school (about 25 children attend; education through age 14 is obligatory). High-schoolers go to the "big city," La Spezia. The red building to the right of the schoolhouse, a former monastery, is the city hall. Vernazza and Corniglia function as one community. Through most of the 1990s, the local government was Communist. In 1999, residents elected a coalition of many parties working to rise above ideologies and simply make Vernazza a better place. That practical notion of government continues here today.

Finally, on the top of the hill, with the best view of all, is the town cemetery. It's only fair that hardworking Vernazzans—who spend their lives climbing up and down and up and down and up and down the hillsides that hem in their little town—are rewarded with a world-class view for eternity.

Activities in Vernazza

Tuesday-Morning Market
Vernazza's skimpy business community is augmented Tuesday mornings (8:00-13:00), when a meager gang of cars and trucks pulls into town for a tailgate market.

Beaches
The harbor's sandy cove has sunning rocks and showers by the breakwater. There's also a ladder on the breakwater for deep-water access. The sunbathing lane directly under the church also has a shower. And don't miss Vernazza's "new beach," accessed through a hole halfway along its main drag (and described on my self-guided walk, earlier). Note that this beach may be closed periodically for safety reasons. It's safer to hang out closer to the water instead of directly under the cliffs, which experience occasional, minor landslides.

Boat Trips
Vincenzo of **Nord Est** takes people out for mini-cruises (€150/hour, mobile 338-700-0436, info@manuela-vernazza.com). One popular stop is the tiny *acqua pendente* (waterfall) cove between Vernazza and Monterosso; locals call it their *laguna blu*.

Shuttle Bus Joyride
For a cheap and scenic joyride, with a chance to chat about the region with friendly, English-speaking Beppe, Simone, or Pietro, ride the shuttle bus from the top of town (in front of the post office) to the sanctuaries and hamlets San Bernadino and Reggio—the ancient birthplace of Vernazza—and back again (entire route for the cost of a round-trip ticket, generally about 5/day, but times are very unpredictable—try asking at the TI or park office in the train station, or if you see a bus, flag it down and ask for the timetable; €2.50 round-trip, free with Cinque Terre Park Card, churches at sanctuaries are usually closed).

Sustainable Tourism Activities
Save Vernazza, which began as a post-flood relief organization, has now evolved into an all-purpose Vernazza advocacy group, with an emphasis on fostering sustainable tourism. They coordinate "voluntourism" activities regularly through the summer (generally May-July and Sept-Oct, 2/week—usually Wed/Thu and Sat/Sun, 8:30-13:30). If you enjoy the Cinque Terre and would like to give something back, contact them to see if you can join a group working on a project designed to protect and promote traditional Vernazzan lifestyles (www.savevernazza.com, workwithus@savevernazza.com, mobile 349-357-3572).

CINQUE TERRE

Nightlife in Vernazza

Vernazza's younger generation of restaurant workers lets loose after-hours. They work hard through the tourist season, travel in the winter, speak English, and enjoy connecting with international visitors. After the restaurants close down, the town is quiet except for a couple of nightspots. For more information on the Blue Marlin, Ananasso, Il Pirata, and Ristorante Incadasè, see their listings under "Eating in Vernazza," later. All Vernazza bars must close by 24:00.

Blue Marlin Bar dominates the late-night scene with a mix of locals and tourists, home-cooked food until 23:00, good drinks, and piano jam sessions. If you're young and hip, this is *the* place to hang out. If you play piano, you're welcome to contribute to the scene. They also host a free book-swap shelf.

Ananasso Bar offers early-evening happy-hour fun and cocktails *(aperitivi)* that both locals and visitors enjoy. Its harborfront tables get the last sunshine of the day.

Burgus Wine Bar, chic and cool with a jazzy ambience, is a popular early-evening and after-dinner harborside hangout, where you can sip local wine or a cocktail (Wed-Mon 7:30-24:00, closed Tue, Piazza Marconi 4).

Il Pirata delle Cinque Terre, behind and above the train station, features the entertaining Cannoli brothers and their devoted tourist clientele. Many come for dinner and end up staying because of these two wild and crazy guys and the camaraderie they create among their diners (erratic hours driven by demand, free Wi-Fi).

Ristorante Incadasè da Piva (tucked up the lane behind the pharmacy) is the haunt of Piva, Vernazza's troubadour. Piva often gets out his guitar and sings traditional local songs as well as his own compositions. If you're looking for a local Hemingway, check here.

Really Late: There's a little cave on the beach just under the church that lends itself to fun in the wee hours, when everything else is closed.

Sleeping in Vernazza

Vernazza, the spindly and salty essence of the Cinque Terre, is my top choice for a home base. Off-season (Oct-March), you can generally arrive without a reservation and find a place, but at other times, it's smart to book ahead (especially June-July and weekends).

People recommended here are listed for their communication skills (they speak English, have email, and are reliable with bookings) and because they rent several rooms. Consequently, my recommendations cost more than comparable rooms you'll find if

CINQUE TERRE

you shop around. Comparison-shopping will likely save you €10-20 per double per night—and often get you a better place and view to boot. The real Vernazza gems are stray single rooms with owners who have no interest in booking in advance or messing with email. Arrive by early afternoon and drop by any shop or bar and ask; most locals know someone who rents rooms.

Anywhere you stay here requires some climbing, but keep in mind that more climbing means better views. Most do not include breakfast (for suggestions, see "Eating in Vernazza," later). Cash is preferred or required almost everywhere. Night noise can be a problem if you're near the station. Rooms on the harbor come with church bells (but only between 7:00 and 22:00).

Pensions

$$$ Trattoria Gianni rents 27 small rooms and three apartments just under the castle. The rooms are in three buildings—one funky, two modern—up a hundred tight, winding spiral stairs. The funky ones, which may or may not have private baths, are artfully decorated à la shipwreck, with tiny balconies and grand sea views *(con vista sul mare)*. The comfy new *(nuovo)* rooms lack views. Both have modern bathrooms and access to a super-scenic cliff-hanging guests' garden. Steely Marisa requires check-in before 16:00 or a phone call to explain when you're coming. Emanuele (Gianni's son, who now runs the restaurant), Simona, Catarina, and the staff speak a little English (S-€55, D-€100, Db-€120, Tb-€150, includes breakfast on their gorgeous seaview terrace mid-April-mid-Oct, prices are lower at other times, 10 percent discount when you pay cash and mention this book—request when you reserve, cancellations less than a week in advance are charged one night's deposit, closed Jan-Feb, Piazza Marconi 1, tel. 0187-812-228, tel. 0187-821-003, on Wed call mobile 393-9008-155 instead, www.giannifranzi.it, info@giannifranzi.it). Pick up your keys at Trattoria Gianni's restaurant on the harbor square (on Wed, when the restaurant is closed, call ahead to make other arrangements).

$$$ Pensione Sorriso, the oldest pension in town (where I stayed on my first visit in 1975), rents 19 overpriced rooms above the train station. While the main building has the charm, it comes with train noise and saggy beds; the annex, up the street, is in a quieter apartment that feels forgotten (Sb-€65, D-€70, Db-€110, Db with air-con-€120, T-€90, Tb-€140, breakfast-€15, free Wi-Fi, closed Nov-March, Via Gavino 4, tel. 0187-812-224, www.

pensionesorriso.com, info@pensionesorriso.com, Francesca and Aldo).

$$ Albergo Barbara rents nine basic rooms overlooking the harbor square—most with small windows and small views. It's run by English-speaking Giuseppe and his no-nonsense Swiss wife, Patricia (D-€55, D with private bath down the hall-€65, Db-€70, big Db with nice harbor view-€110, extra bed-€10, 2-night stay preferred, closed Dec-Feb, reserve online with credit card but pay cash, free Wi-Fi, Piazza Marconi 30, tel. 0187-812-398, mobile 338-793-3261, www.albergobarbara.it, info@albergobarbara.it).

Private Rooms *(Affitta Camere)*

Vernazza is honeycombed with private rooms, offering the best values in town. Owners may be reluctant to reserve rooms far in advance. Doubles cost €55-100, depending on the view, season, and plumbing—you get what you pay for. Apartments (with kitchens) go for a bit more. Most places accept only cash. Some have killer views, come with lots of stairs, and cost the same as a small, dark place on a back lane over the train tracks. Most of these people speak just enough English (or know someone who does).

While a few places have all their beds in one building, most have rooms scattered over town. Better-organized outfits have an informal "reception desk" (sometimes at a restaurant or other business) where you can check in. A few places have no reception at all. (On the Vernazza map, I've marked only places that have a fixed address or reception office; if I say "reception," you'll check in there, then continue on to your actual room.) Because this can be confusing, I strongly recommend clearly communicating your arrival time (by phone or email) and getting clear instructions on where to meet the owner and pick up the keys. In many cases, they'll meet you at the train station—but only if they know when you're coming.

Well-Run Rooms in the Inland Part of Town

Some of my favorite places in town are located in the ravine a five-minute, gently uphill stroll behind the train station. While this sleepy zone is less atmospheric and feels less central than Vernazza's main street, harborfront, and twisty upper lanes, it also has less train and church-bell noise and fewer steep stairs. While none of these places have views, the constant soundtrack of Vernazza's gurgling river is soothing. Il Pirata delle Cinque Terre is the neighborhood hub (offering breakfast and Wi-Fi), and Vernazza's self-service launderette is right next door.

$$$ Alessandra runs two different sets of rooms in a single elevator-equipped, modern building: **La Perla delle 5 Terre** (6 clean, sleek rooms with modern style but no air-con, Db-€100, Tb-€120) and **Tonino Basso** (4 rooms decorated with big colorful cutouts,

Db-€120, Tb-€140, air-con, loaner laptop in each room). This is the top choice in town for modern comfort—at a steep price. Both come with free Wi-Fi; La Perla is a better value if you don't need air-conditioning (contact for both: Via Gavino 34, mobile 339-761-1651, www.toninobasso.com, sassarinialessandra@libero.it).

$$ Camere Fontana Vecchia, run by Annamaria, has eight bright, spacious, quiet rooms overlooking the ravine and its rushing river, across the street from the post office (D-€70, Db-€80, Db with terrace-€100, Via Gavino 15, tel. 0187-821-130, mobile 333-454-9371, www.cinqueterrecamere.com, m.annamaria@libero.it).

$$ Giuliano Basso's four carefully crafted rooms are just above town, straddling a ravine among orange trees. It's proudly built out of stone by Giuliano himself—the town's last stone-layer (Db-€80-100, Tb-€120, two rooms have air-con, more train noise than others, above train station, take the ramp just before Pensione Sorriso, mobile 333-341-4792, www.cdh.it/giuliano, giuliano@cdh.it).

Other Reliable Places Scattered Through Town and the Harborside

La Malà, La Marina Rooms, and Memo Rooms are not located on the map in this chapter; arrange a meeting time and/or ask for directions when you reserve.

$$$ La Malà is Vernazza's jetsetter pad. Four pristine white rooms boast fancy-hotel-type extras and a common terrace looking out over the rocky shore. It's a climb—way, way up to the top of town—but they'll gladly carry your bags to and from the station (Db-€160, Db suite-€220, includes breakfast at a bar, air-con, free Wi-Fi, mobile 334-287-5718, www.lamala.it, info@lamala.it, charming Giamba and his mama, Armanda). They also rent the simpler "Armanda's Room" nearby—a great value, since you get Giamba's attention to detail and amenities without paying for a big view (Db-€80, includes simple breakfast in room, air-con, book through La Malà or ring bell at Piazza Marconi 15).

$$$ La Marina Rooms is run by hardworking Christian, who speaks English and happily meets his guests at the station to carry their bags. There are five beautiful, top-end, pricey units, most high above the main street: Three doubles share a fine oceanview terrace (townview Db-€90, seaview Db-€140), and two apartments are more spacious, with fine terraces and views (townview Db-€120, seaview Db with big terrace-€260; mobile 338-476-7472, www.lamarinarooms.com, mapcri@yahoo.it).

$$$ Martina Callo's four simply furnished rooms overlook the square; they're up plenty of steps near the silent-at-night church tower. While the rooms are nothing special, guests appreciate the views (room #1: Tb-€110 or Qb-€120 with harbor view; room #2:

big Qb family room with no view-€110; room #3: Db with grand view terrace-€100; room #4: roomy Db with no view-€60; air-con, free Wi-Fi, ring bell at Piazza Marconi 26, tel. 0187-812-365, mobile 329-435-5344, www.roomartina.com, roomartina@roomartina.com).

$$ Memo Rooms has three clean and spacious rooms that offer good value. They overlook the main street, in what feels like a miniature hotel. Enrica will meet you if you call upon arrival (Db-€70, Via Roma 15, tel. 0187-812-360 but try mobile first, mobile 338-285-2385, www.memorooms.com, info@memorooms.com).

$$ Monica Lercari rents several classy rooms with modern comforts, perched at the top of town. Guests are welcome to borrow the family rowboat or mountain bike (small Db-€80, seaview D-€100, grand seaview terrace D-€120; the previous two rooms can be booked as one big "honeymoon suite" for €180; includes breakfast, air-con, free Wi-Fi, tel. 0187-812-296, mobile 320-025-4515, alcastellovernazza@yahoo.it). For years Monica and her husband, Massimo, had one of Vernazza's most scenic, memorable, and inviting restaurants, Ristorante al Castello, in the old castle tower overlooking town; damaged in the flood, it may reopen in the future—ask around, or try calling tel. 0187-812-296.

$$ Nicolina Rooms consists of seven units in three different buildings. Two rooms are in the center over the pharmacy, up a few steep steps—one has only sleeper sofas (Db-€80-90); another room is on a twisty lane above the harbor (Db-€80); and four more are in a building beyond the church, with great views (D-€100, Db-€140, two-bedroom suite with harborview terrace-€180 plus €30/extra person, free Wi-Fi and loud church bells in these rooms only). Inquire at Pizzeria Vulnetia on the harbor square (all include breakfast, Piazza Marconi 29, tel. 0187-821-193, mobile 333-842-6879, www.camerenicolina.it, camerenicolina.info@cdh.it).

$$ Rosa Vitali rents two four-person apartments across from the pharmacy overlooking the main street (and beyond the train noise). One has a terrace and fridge (top floor); the other has windows and a full kitchen (Db-€85, Tb-€110, Qb-€120, reception just before the tobacco shop near Piazza Marconi at Via Visconti 10, tel. 0187-821-181, mobile 340-267-5009, www.rosacamere.it, rosa.vitali@libero.it).

$$ Francamaria and her kind husband Andrea rent eight sharp, comfortable, and creatively renovated but expensive rooms—all described in detail on her website. While their reception desk is on the harbor square (on the ground floor facing the harbor at Piazza Marconi 30—don't confuse it with Albergo Barbara at same address), the rooms they manage are all over town (Db-€80-120 depending on size and view, Qb-€130-160, extra person-€20, tel. 0187-812-002, mobile 328-711-9728, www.francamaria.com, info@francamaria.com).

More Private Rooms in Vernazza

Rooms from Emanuela Colombo, Maria Capellini, and Manuela Moggia are not located on the map in this chapter; arrange a meeting time and/or ask for directions when you reserve.

$$ Vernazza Rooms, run by Daria Bianchi, Chiara, and Davide, rents 13 decent rooms: Five are above the Blue Marlin Bar looking down on the main street, and eight are a steep climb higher up, just under the city hall (Db-€60-95, Qb-€100-120; price depends on view, location, and size; ring bell at Via Roma 41—next to Blue Marlin Bar, some with air-con and others with fans, free Wi-Fi in some rooms, mobile 338-581-4688 or 338-413-8696, www.vernazzarooms.com, info@vernazzarooms.com).

$$ Emanuela Colombo has two rooms—one spacious and basic on the harbor square (Db-€85), the other a *molto* chic split-level apartment located on a quiet side street (Db-€100, Tb-€120; tel. 339-834-2486, www.vacanzemanuela.it, manucap64@libero.it).

$$ Rooms Francesca's three rooms hide out in the steep streets just below the city hall (non-view Db-€70, seaview Db-€80, non-view Tb-€90, 2-room apartment: Db-€90/Qb-€120; check in at Enoteca Sciacchetrà at Via Roma 19, tel. 0187-821-112, www.5terre-vernazza.it, moggia.franco@libero.it, Francesca and Franco).

$$ Ivo's Camere rents two simple no-terrace rooms high above the main street, as well as a studio apartment (Db-€75, air-con, free Wi-Fi, Via Roma 6, reception at Pizzeria Fratelli Basso—Via Roma 1, mobile 333-477-5521, www.ivocamere.com, post@ivocamere.com).

$$ Maria Capellini rents a couple of simple, clean rooms, including one on the ground floor right on the harbor (Db with kitchen-€90, Tb-€110, cash only, fans, mobile 338-436-3411, www.mariacapellini.com, mariacapellini@hotmail.it, Maria and Giacomo).

More Options: **$$ Affitta Camere Alberto Basso** (a clean, modern room with a noisy harbor/piazza view, Db-€80, check in at Internet Point, albertobasso@hotmail.com); **$$ Capitano Rooms** (3 recently remodeled rooms up several flights of stairs above the main drag, Db-€90, includes breakfast, fans, free Wi-Fi at restaurant; ask for Julia, Paolo, or Barbara at the Trattoria del Capitano restaurant on the main square at Piazza Marconi 21; tel. 0187-812-201, www.tavernavernazza.com, info@tavernavernazza.com); **$$ Eva's Rooms** (3 rooms overlooking main street, Sb-€60, D with private bath outside the room-€70, Db-€80, air-con, train noise, ring at Via Roma 56, tel. 0187-821-134, www.evasrooms. it, evasrooms@yahoo.it); **$$ Manuela Moggia** (4 rooms, Db-€80, Db with kitchen or view-€100, Tb-€95, Tb with kitchen or view-€110, Qb with kitchen-€125, some behind the train station at Via Gavino 22, tel. 0187-812-397, mobile 333-413-6374, www.man-uela-vernazza.com, info@manuela-vernazza.com); and **$$ Rooms Elisabetta** (3 tight, tired, simple, casually run rooms at the tip-top of town with Vernazza's ultimate 360-degree roof terrace—come here only for the views, Db-€70, Tb-€95, Qb-€110, these prices if you book direct and pay cash, fans, free Wi-Fi, partway up the Corniglia path at Via Carattino 62, mobile 347-451-1834, www. elisabettacarro.it, carroelisabetta@hotmail.com, Elisabetta and dad Pino).

Eating in Vernazza

Breakfast

Locals take breakfast about as seriously as flossing. A cappuccino and a pastry or a piece of focaccia from a bar or bakery does it. Most of my recommended accommodations don't come with breakfast (when they do, I've noted so in my listings). Assuming you're on your own, you have four basic options: Blue Marlin Bar for its extensive menu, including bacon and eggs; Il Pirata delle Cinque Terre for sugary stuff and a lively welcome; Ananasso Bar for coffee and a sweet roll on the harborfront; or any bakery for picnic goodies.

Blue Marlin Bar (mid-town, just below the train station) serves a good array of clearly priced à la carte items including eggs and bacon (only after 8:45), adding up to the priciest breakfast in town (likely to total €10). It's run by Massimo and Carmen with the capable assistance of Jeff, an American who now lives in Vernazza. If you're awaiting a train any time of day, the Blue Marlin's outdoor seating beats the platform (Thu-Tue 7:00-24:00, closed Wed).

Il Pirata delle Cinque Terre, an endearing tourist trap, is located in the workaday zone behind and above the train station. The dynamic Sicilian duo Gianluca and Massimo (hardworking twins, a.k.a. the Cannoli brothers) enthusiastically offer a wide assortment of Sicilian pastries. Their fun, playful service makes up for the lack of a view. Massimo is a likeable loudmouth, while Gianluca is a pastry artist, hand-painting fanciful sculptured marzipan. Their sweet pastry breakfasts include an array of treats like *panzerotto* (made of ricotta, cinnamon, and vanilla, €2.50) and hot cheese and pesto bruschetta (€3). They proudly serve no bacon and eggs (since "this is Italy"). While the atmosphere of the place seems like suburban Milan, it has a curious charisma among its customers—bringing Vernazza a welcome bit of Sicily (daily 6:30-24:00, Via Gavino 36, tel. 0187-812-047).

Ananasso Bar feels Old World, with youthful energy and a great location with little tables right on the harbor. They offer toasted *panini,* pastries, and designer cappuccino. You can eat a bit cheaper at the bar (you're welcome to picnic on the nearby bench or seawall rocks with a Mediterranean view) or enjoy the best-situated tables in town (Fri-Wed 8:00-late, closed Thu).

Picnic Breakfast: Drop by one of Vernazza's several little bakeries, focaccia shops, or grocery stores to assemble a breakfast to eat on the breakwater. Top it off with a coffee in a nearby bar.

Lunch and Dinner

If you enjoy Italian cuisine and seafood, Vernazza's restaurants are worth the splurge. All take pride in their cooking. Wander around at about 20:00 and compare the ambience, but don't wait too late to eat—many kitchens close at 22:00. (Immigrants, who are doing more and more of the hard work of cooking and cleaning, need to wrap things up in time to catch the last train back to La Spezia, where many of them live.) To get an outdoor table on summer weekends, reserve ahead. Expect to spend around €10-12 for pastas, €12-16 for *secondi,* and €2-3 for a cover charge. Harborside restaurants and bars are easygoing. You're welcome to grab a cup of coffee or glass of wine and disappear somewhere on the breakwater, returning your glass when you're done. If you dine in Vernazza but are staying in another town, be sure to check train schedules before sitting down to eat, as trains run less frequently in the evening. Anchovies (prepared in a dizzying variety of ways) are the specialty. Any restaurant loves to show off with dazzling *antipasti misti* plates of seafood and anchovies.

Harborside

Gambero Rosso ("Red Prawn," the same name as Italy's top restaurant guide) is considered Vernazza's best-regarded restaurant... and charges accordingly. It feels dressier than the others. Try Chef Claudio's namesake risotto, *riso alla Cla* (€10-16 pastas, €16-25 *secondi,* Fri-Wed 12:00-15:30 & 19:00-22:00, closed Thu and Dec-Feb, Piazza Marconi 7, tel. 0187-812-265).

Trattoria Gianni is an old standby for locals and tourists who appreciate the best prices on the harbor, without sacrificing quality cuisine. You'll enjoy well-prepared seafood and receive steady, reliable, and friendly service from Emanuele and Alessandro. Ask about their off-menu specials. While the outdoor seating is basic, the indoor setting is classy (€10-15 pastas, €9-15 *secondi* plus a few €22-24 splurges, check their *menù cucina tipica Vernazza,* Thu-Tue

12:00-15:00 & 19:00-22:00, closed Wed except July-Aug, tel. 0187-812-228).

Trattoria del Capitano, a slightly more affordable option on the square, serves a short menu of straightforward local dishes, including €12 *spaghetti con frutti di mare*—pasta entangled with various types of seafood and €20 *grigliata mista*—a mix of seasonal Mediterranean fish (€8-12 pastas, €15-18 *secondi*, Wed-Mon 12:00-15:00 & 19:00-22:00, closed Tue except in Aug, closed Nov-Dec, tel. 0187-812-201, Paolo speaks English, grandpa Giacomo doesn't need to).

Ristorante Pizzeria Vulnetia is simpler, serving regional specialties such as prizewinning *tegame alla Vernazzana*—anchovies, tomatoes, and potatoes baked in the oven. They also offer pizzas—unlike the three places listed above—making this a good choice for a group with differing tastes (€7-10 pizzas, €8-13 pastas, €12-18 *secondi*, Tue-Sun 12:00-15:30 & 18:30-22:00, closed Mon, Piazza Marconi 29, tel. 0187-821-193, Giuliano).

Pizzeria Baia Saracena ("Saracen Bay") is the only budget option on the harbor, serving pizza and pastas out on the breakwater. Eat here not for high cuisine, but for memorable atmosphere at reasonable prices (€5-9 salads, €9 pizzas and pastas, Sat-Thu 10:30-22:00, closed Fri, tel. 0187-812-113, Luca).

Above the Harbor, by the Castle

Ristorante Belforte's experimental, beautifully presented, creative cuisine includes a hearty *zuppa Michela* (€25 for a boatload of seafood), fishy *spaghetti alla Bruno* (€13), and *trofie al pesto* (hand-rolled noodles with pesto, €15). Their classic *antipasti misto di pesce* (€18 for five plates) can be shared by two people. From the breakwater, follow either the stairs or the rope that leads up and around to the restaurant. You'll find a web of tables embedded in four levels of the lower part of the old castle. For the ultimate seaside perch, call and reserve one of four tables on the *terrazza con vista* (view terrace). Most of Belforte's seating is outdoors—if the weather's bad, the interior can get crowded (€13-16 pastas, €22-28 *secondi*, Wed-Mon 12:00-15:00 & 19:00-22:00, closed Tue and Nov-March, tel. 0187-812-222, Michela).

Inland, on or near the Main Street

Several of Vernazza's inland eateries manage to compete without the harbor ambience, but with slightly cheaper prices.

Trattoria da Sandro, on the main drag, mixes Genovese and Ligurian cuisine with friendly service. It can be a peaceful alternative to the harborside scene. They take pride in their food, and dish up award-winning stuffed mussels (€8-13 pastas, €13-18 *secondi*,

Wed-Mon 12:00-15:00 & 18:30-22:00, closed Tue, Via Roma 62, tel. 0187-812-223, Gabriella and Alessandro).

Antica Osteria il Baretto is another solid bet for homey, reasonably priced traditional cuisine, run by Simone and Jenny. As it's off the harbor and a little less glitzy than the others, it's favored by locals who prefer less noisy English while they eat great homemade fish ravioli. Sitting deep in their interior can be a peaceful escape (€9-14 pasta, €10-18 *secondi,* Tue-Sat 12:00-22:00, closed Mon, indoor and outdoor seating, Via Roma 31, tel. 0187-812-381).

Ristorante Incadasè da Piva is a rare bit of old Vernazza. For 25 years, charismatic Piva has been known for his *tegame Vernazza,* his *riso Piva* (seafood risotto), and his love of music. The town troubadour, he often serenades his guests when the cooking's done. Piva is now joined by his son, Raphael, who speaks English. *Incadasè* is local dialect for (roughly) "a weary sailor returning home from a long voyage" (€8-13 pastas, €14-18 *secondi,* Fri-Wed 12:00-15:00 & 19:00-22:00, closed Thu, tucked away 20 yards off the main drag, up a lane behind the pharmacy, tel. 0187-812-194).

Other Eating Options

Blue Marlin Bar (on the main street and described under "Breakfast," earlier) busts out of the Vernazzan-cuisine rut with a short, creative menu of more casual dishes. It's a good choice if you just want to grab some reliable food rather than dine. Locals enjoy a meal here when they don't feel like cooking at home (€6-8 pizzas, €9-10 pastas, €10-12 *secondi,* closed Wed).

Il Pirata delle Cinque Terre, popular for breakfast, also attracts many travelers for lunch and dinner (€8-10 pastas, €7-9 salads). Don't come here for the cuisine or for the ambience (it's a simple café/pastry shop), but for a memorable evening with the Cannoli twins, who entertain while they serve, as diners enjoy their meals while laughing out loud. The menu, aimed squarely at American tourists' taste buds, offers a break from more authentic Ligurian fare (at the top of town; for complete description, see listing under "Breakfast," earlier).

Pizzerias, Sandwiches, and Groceries: Vernazza's main-street eateries offer a fine range of quick meals. Two **pizzerias** stay busy, and while they mostly do takeout, each will let you sit and eat for the same cheap price. One has tables on the street, and the other, called Ercole, hides a tiny terrace and a few tables out back. **Forno Bakery** has good focaccia and veggie tarts (at #3), and several bars sell sandwiches and pizza by the slice. **Pino's grocery store** also makes inexpensive sandwiches to order (generally Mon-Sat 8:00-13:00 & 17:00-19:30, closed Sun). Tiny jars of pesto spread give elegance to picnics.

Gelato: The town has three *gelaterias:* **Gelateria Vernazza,**

near the top of the main street, takes its gelato seriously, occasionally flirting with creative ingredients (soy) and flavors (*riso*—rice, and ricotta and fig). What looks like **Gelateria Amore Mio** (midtown) is actually Gelateria Stalin—founded in 1968 by a pastry chef with that unfortunate name (now it's run by his niece Sonia and nephew Francesco, with great people-watching tables but the least exciting gelato in town). And out on the harbor, the aptly named **Gelateria Il Porticciolo** ("Marina") is arguably the best; they use fresh ingredients to create intense flavors (try their *cannella*—cinnamon, or their *nocciola*—hazelnut).

Monterosso al Mare (Town #5)

This is a resort with a few cars and lots of hotels, rentable beach umbrellas, crowds, and a little more late-night action than the neighboring towns. Monterosso al Mare—the only Cinque Terre town built on flat land—has two parts: A new town (called Fegina) with a parking lot, train station, and TI; and an old town (Centro Storico), which cradles Old World charm in its small, crooked lanes. In the old town, you'll find hole-in-the-wall shops, pastel townscapes, and a new generation of creative small-businesspeople eager to keep their visitors happy.

A pedestrian tunnel connects the old with the new, but take a small detour around the point for a nicer walk. It offers a close-up view of two sights: a 16th-century lookout tower, built after the last serious pirate raid in 1545; and a Nazi "pillbox," a small, low concrete bunker where gunners hid. (During World War II, nearby La Spezia was an important Axis naval base, and Monterosso was bombed while the Germans were here.)

Strolling the waterfront promenade, you can pick out each of the Cinque Terre towns decorating the coast. After dark, they sparkle. Monterosso is the most enjoyable of the five for young travelers wanting to connect with others looking for a little evening action. Even so, Monterosso is not a full-blown Portofino-style resort—and locals appreciate quiet, sensitive guests.

Monterosso sustained serious damage in the 2011 flood, but within just a few months, it was back up and running at nearly 100 percent. Walking through the town today, you'll have to know where to look to find evidence of the devastation. Big grates on the six roads cover the historic canals (which drain runoff from the surrounding hills into the sea), and the sound of rushing water reassures townsfolk that the streams are flowing unimpeded below.

Orientation to Monterosso

Tourist Information
The TI Proloco is next to the train station (April-Oct daily 9:00-19:00, closed Nov-March, exit station and go left a few doors, tel. 0187-817-506, www.prolocomonterosso.it). For national park tickets and information, head upstairs within the station to the ticket office near platform 1 (likely daily 7:00-19:00, shorter hours off-season). If you arrive late on a summer day, the old town's Internet café is helpful with tourist information (see later).

Rebuild Monterosso: Led by a group of American women who married into the community, Rebuild Monterosso brought relief to the town in the immediate aftermath of the flood and has since evolved into an organization focused on fostering healthy tourism and keeping visitors up to date on the latest in town (www.rebuildmonterosso.com).

Arrival in Monterosso
By Train: Train travelers arrive in the new town, from which it's a scenic, flat 10-minute stroll to all the old town action (leave station to the left; to reach hotels in the new town, turn right out of station). The bar at track 1, which overlooks both the tracks and the beach, is a handy place to hang out while waiting for your train to pull in (salads, sandwiches, drinks). As many trains run late, this can turn a frustration into a blessing.

Shuttle buses run roughly hourly along the waterfront between the old town (Piazza Garibaldi, just beyond the tunnel), the train station, and the parking lot at the end of Via Fegina (*Campo Sportivo* stop). While the buses can be convenient—saving you a 10-minute schlep with your bags—they only go once an hour, and are likely not worth the trouble (€1.50, free with Cinque Terre Park Card).

The other alternative is to take a **taxi** (certain vehicles have permission to drive in the old city center). They usually wait outside the train station, but you may have to call (€7 from station to the old town, mobile 335-616-5842 or 335-628-0933).

By Car: Monterosso is 30 minutes off the freeway (exit: Carrodano-Levanto). Note that about three miles above Monterosso, a fork directs you to either *Centro Storico* (old part of town—Via Roma parking lot with a few spots, and possibly the new Loreto garage) or *Fegina* (the new town and beachfront parking, most likely where you want to go). At this point you must choose which area, because you can't drive directly from the new town to the old center (which is closed to cars without special permits).

Parking is easy (except July-Aug and summer weekends) in the huge beachfront guarded lot in the new town (€18/24 hours). If you're heading to the old town, you'll find the Loreto parking garage on Via Roma, a 10-minute downhill walk to the main square (€1.70/hour, €18/24 hours). For the cheapest Monterosso rates, park along the blue lines (a few minutes farther uphill from the Loreto garage) for €8 per day. See "Cinque Terre Connections" at the end of this chapter for directions from Milan and tips on driving in the Cinque Terre.

Helpful Hints

Thursday Morning Market: Every Thursday morning, trucks pull into the old town and fill the public area by the beach with temporary stalls where locals get the items not otherwise available in this small town.

Medical Help: The town's bike-riding, leather bag-toting, English-speaking physician is **Dr. Vitone,** who charges €50-80 for a simple visit (less for poor students, mobile 338-853-0949).

Internet Access: The Net, a few steps off the old town's main drag (Via Roma), has six high-speed computers (€1/10 minutes) and Wi-Fi (a bit cheaper). Enzo happily provides information on the Cinque Terre, rents rooms (see "Sleeping in Monterosso," later), and can burn your photos onto a DVD for €6 (daily 9:30-23:00, off-season closes at 19:00, Via Vittorio Emanuele 55, tel. 0187-817-288, www.monterossonet.com, info@monterossonet.com).

Baggage Storage: Wash and Dry Lavarapido, two blocks from the station, provides a wonderful bag-check service. Just drop off your bag for €5 (details in next listing).

Laundry: For full-service laundry in the new town, **Wash and Dry Lavarapido** will return your laundry to your hotel (€12/13 pounds, daily 8:00-19:00, Via Molinelli 17, mobile 339-484-0940, Lucia and Ivano).

Boat Trips: Stefano or **Nico** can take you on a cruise around the Cinque Terre (€100/hour, one hour is enough for a quick spin, two hours includes time for swimming stops; longer trips to Portovenere and offshore islands also possible). Stefano's slower boat, *Matilde,* holds up to 6 people, while Nico's fast boat, *Il Delfino,* takes up to 10 and also does taxi boat transfers (€50 one-way to Monterosso, €80 one-way to Riomaggiore, €300 to Portovenere; Stefano's mobile 333-821-2007, Nico's mobile 345-424-9015, www.matildenavigazione.com, info@matildenavigazione.com).

Monterosso al Mare

To Levanto &
Autostrada
Exit: Carrodano-
Levanto

Not to Scale

Walk from Train Station
to Piazza Garibaldi
is approx. 10 mins.

VIA PADRE SEM.

VIA MESCO

VIA PADRE SEM.

VIA MOLINELLI

NEW TOWN
(FEGINA)

TRAIN
STATION

VIA NOV.

VIA E. MONTALE

VIA FEGINA

Beach

Trail to
Levanto

Beach
(Free)

Beach
(Free)

IL GIGANTE
STATUE

BREAKWATER

Ligurian

❶ Hotel Villa Steno	❽ Manuel's Guesthouse	⓮ Hotel la Spiaggia
❷ Albergo Pasquale	❾ Buranco Agriturismo	⓯ Hotel Punta Mesco
❸ Locanda il Maestrale	❿ Albergo al Carugio	⓰ Pensione Agavi
❹ Il Giardino Incanto	⓫ The Net (Rooms)	⓱ Affittacamere Rist. Il
❺ L'Antica Terrazza	& Pizzeria la Smorfia	Gabbiano
❻ Albergo Marina	⓬ A Cà du Gigante	⓲ Le Sirene/Raggi
❼ Hotel la Colonnina	⓭ Hotel Villa Adriana	di Sole

Massage: Giorgio Moggia, the local physiotherapist, gives good
massages at your hotel or in his studio (€60/hour, tel. 339-314-
6127, giomogg@tin.it).

Self-Guided Walk

Welcome to Monterosso

This walk will introduce you to Monterosso, beginning with an
easy and lazy sweep of the head from the breakwater. Part 1, focus-
ing on the mostly level town center, takes about 30 minutes; for
Part 2, summiting the adjacent hill, allow another hour or so.

19 Ristorante Belvedere
20 Il Casello
21 Ristorante Tortuga
22 Via Venti Restaurant
23 Ristorante al Pozzo
24 Ciak Restaurant
25 L'Alta Marea Rist.

26 Miky Restaurant
27 La Cantina di Miky
28 Il Frantoio Focacceria
29 Focacceria da Emy
30 Il Massimo della Foccacia
31 Enoteca Eliseo

32 Fast Bar
33 Nuovo Eden Bar
34 Laundry & Bag Check

Part 1: Monterosso Harbor and Town Center

• *Hike out from the dock in the old town and climb five rough steps to the very top of the concrete...*

Breakwater: If you're visiting by boat, you'll start here anyway. From this point you can survey Monterosso's old town (straight ahead) and new town (stretching to the left, with train station and parking lot). Notice the bluff that separates old and new, and imagine how much harder your commute would be if the narrow road tethering these two towns were somehow cut off. It happened in the spring of 2013, when the wall below the Capuchin church (at the top of the hill) gave way, creating a landslide. For a time, the only ways to connect the two halves of town were to drive six miles around...or hike up and over this hill. (The little fort halfway up the hill, which dates from 1550, is now a private home.)

Looking to the right, you can actually see all *cinque* of the *terre* from one spot: Vernazza, Corniglia (above the shore), Manarola, and a few buildings of Riomaggiore beyond that.

These days, the harbor hosts more paddleboats than fishing boats. Sand erosion is a major problem. The partial breakwater (a row of giant rocks in the middle of the harbor) is designed to save the beach from washing away. While old-timers remember a vast beach, their grandchildren truck in sand each spring to give tourists something to lie on. (The Nazis liked the Cinque Terre, too—find two of their bomb-hardened bunkers, near left and far right.)

The fancy €300-a-night, four-star Hotel Porto Roca (pink building high on the hill, on the far right of the harbor) marks the trail to Vernazza. High above, you see an example of the costly roads built in the 1980s to connect the Cinque Terre towns with the freeway over the hills.

The two prominent capes (Punta di Montenero to the right, and Punta Mesco to the left) define the Cinque Terre region. The closer cape, Punta Mesco, marks an important sea-life sanctuary, home to a rare sea grass that provides an ideal home for fish eggs. Buoys keep fishing boats away. The cape was once a quarry, providing employment to locals who chipped out the stones used to build the local towns (the greenish stones making up part of the breakwater below you are from there).

On the far end of the new town, marking the best free beach around, you can just see the statue named *Il Gigante* (hard to spot because it blends in with the gray rock). It's 45 feet tall and once held a trident. While it looks as if it were hewn from the rocky cliff, it's actually made of reinforced concrete and dates from the beginning of the 20th century, when it supported a dancing terrace for a *fin de siècle* villa. A violent storm left the giant holding nothing but memories of Monterosso's glamorous age.

• *From the breakwater, walk into the old town. At the top of the beach, notice the openings of two big drains, ready to let flash floods rip through town without destroying things. Walking under the train tracks, venture right into the square and find the statue of a dandy holding what looks like a box cutter.*

Piazza Garibaldi: The statue honors Giuseppe Garibaldi, the dashing firebrand revolutionary who, in the 1860s, helped unite the people of Italy into a modern nation. Facing Garibaldi, with your back to the sea, you'll see (from right to left) the orange city hall (with the now-required European Union flag beside the Italian one) and a big home and recreation center for poor and homeless elderly. You'll also see A Ca' du Sciensa restaurant (with historic town photos inside and upstairs; you're welcome to pop in for a look).

After the 2011 flood, it was on this square that the National Guard set up an emergency tent, used for staging emergency deliveries, community meals, Christmas Eve Mass, and the New Year's Eve disco. In the aftermath of the flood, many moving stories emerged. Old ladies who couldn't help dig, helped cook. People worried that Laura, whose bakery—loved for her secret recipes—was destroyed, wouldn't be able to reopen. But she rebuilt, and that beautiful aroma of her sweet cakes again helps locals greet each new day. The motorbike of Diego's dreams, which he had bought just 10 days before the flood, was buried by the mud. He excavated it, cleaned it up, and—to the cheers of his friends—it started. The local civil protection unit is now named for 40-year-old volunteer Sandro Usai, Monterosso's one death from the flood. Sandro was last seen heroically trying to open up a grate to increase canal drainage. His body washed ashore a week later, and his funeral was the first time the community stopped working and was silent together. Sandro posthumously received the highest civilian award the Italian government gives.

Just under the bell tower (with your back to the sea, it's on your left), a set of covered arcades facing the sea is where the old-timers hang out (they see all and know all). The crenellated bell tower marks the church.

• Go to church (the entrance is on the inland side).

Church of St. John the Baptist (Chiesa di San Giovanni Battista): Before entering, check out the facade. This black-and-white church, with white marble from Carrara and green marble from Punte Mesco, is typical of this region's Romanesque style. Note the lacy, stone rose window above the entrance. It's as delicate as crochet work, with 18 slender mullions (the petals of the rose). The marble stripes get narrower the higher they go, creating the illusion of a church that's taller than it really is.

Step inside for more Ligurian Gothic: original marble columns and capitals with pointed arches to match. The octagonal baptismal font (in the back of the church) was carved from Carrara marble in 1359. Imagine the job getting that from the quarries to here. In the chapel to the right of the high altar, look for the wooden statue of St. Anthony, carved about 1400, which once graced a church that stood atop Punta Mesco. The church itself dates from 1307—see the proud inscription on the left-middle column: "MilleCCCVII." Outside the church, on the side facing the main street, find the high-water mark from an October 1966 flood (the same month as the flood that devastated Florence). Nearly half a century later, the crippling October 2011 flood hit Monterosso. But the church's statues survived, thanks to townspeople who came to their rescue, carrying them through raging waters to safety. Later, when there was enough help in the streets, excess volunteers came into the church and lovingly polished the candlesticks, just to keep caring for their town.

• *Leaving the church, immediately turn left and go to church again.*

Oratory of the Dead (Oratorio dei Neri): During the Counter-Reformation, the Catholic Church offset the rising influence of the Lutherans by creating brotherhoods of good works. These religious Rotary clubs were called "confraternities." Monterosso had two, nicknamed White and Black. This building is the oratory of the Black group, whose mission—as the macabre decor filling the interior indicates—was to arrange for funerals and take care of widows, orphans, the shipwrecked, and the souls of those who ignore the request for a €1 donation. It dates from the 16th century, and membership has passed from father to son for generations. Notice the fine carved choir stalls (c. 1700) just inside the door, and the haunted-house chandeliers. Look up at the ceiling to find the symbol of the confraternity: a skull-and-crossbones and an hourglass...death awaits us all.

• *On that cheery note, if you're in a lazy mood, you can discreetly split off from our walking tour now to enjoy strolling, shopping, gelato-licking, a day at the beach...or all of the above. But if you're up for a hike, continue with me on Part 2. As you face out to sea, look to the right and imagine the views from the top of that hill. Now...go see them.*

Part 2: Capuchin Church and Hilltop Cemetery

• *Return to the beach and find the brick steps that lead up to the hill-capping convent (starting between the train tracks and the pedestrian tunnel, and passing in front of Albergo Pasquale). Approaching the bend in the path, watch for the stairs leading steeply and sharply to the right. This lane (Salita dei Cappuccini) is nicknamed* Zii di Frati, *or...*

Switchbacks of the Friars: Follow the yellow brick road (OK, it's orange...but I couldn't help singing as I skipped skyward). Pause at the terrace above the castle at a statue of St. Francis and a wolf taking in a grand view. Enjoy another opportunity to see all five of the Cinque Terre towns. From here, backtrack 20 yards and continue uphill.

• *When you reach a gate marked* Convento e Chiesa Cappuccini, *you have arrived at the...*

Church of the Capuchin Friars: The former convent is now manned by a single caretaker friar. Before stepping inside, notice the church's striped Romanesque facade. It's all fake. Tap it—no marble, just cheap 18th-century stucco. Go inside and sit in the rear pew. The high altarpiece painting of St. Francis can be rolled up on special days to reveal a statue of Mary standing behind it. Look at the statue of St. Anthony to the right and smile (you're on convent camera). Wave at the security camera—they're nervous about the precious painting to your left.

This fine painting of the ***Crucifixion*** is attributed to Anthony van Dyck, the 17th-century Flemish master who lived and worked for years in nearby Genoa (though art historians suspect that, at best, it was painted by someone in the artist's workshop). When Jesus died, the earth went dark. Notice the eclipsed sun in the painting, just to the right of the cross. Do the electric candles work? Pick one up, pray for peace, and plug it in. (Leave €0.50, or unplug it and put it back.)

• Leave and turn left to hike 100 yards uphill to the cemetery that fills the remains of the castle, capping the hill. Look back from the gate and enjoy the view over the town.

Cemetery in the Ruined Castle: In the Dark Ages, the village huddled within this castle. Slowly it expanded. Notice the town view from here—no sea. You're looking at the oldest part of Monterosso, tucked behind the hill, out of view of 13th-century pirates. Explore the cemetery, but remember that cemeteries are sacred and treasured places (as is clear by the abundance of fresh flowers). Ponder the black-and-white photos of grandparents past. *Q.R.P.* is *Qui Riposa in Pace* (a.k.a. R.I.P.). Rich families had their own little tomb buildings. Climb to the very summit—the castle's keep, or place of last refuge. Priests are buried in a line of graves closest to the sea, but facing inland, toward the town's holy sanctuary high on the hillside (above the road, with its triangular steeple peeking above the trees). Each Cinque Terre town has a lofty sanctuary, dedicated to Mary and dear to the village hearts.

• From here, your tour is over—any trail leads you back into town.

Sights in Monterosso

Beaches

Monterosso's beaches, immediately in front of the train station, are easily the Cinque Terre's best and most crowded. This town is a sandy resort with rentable beach extras: Figure €20 to rent two chairs and an umbrella for the day. Light lunches are served by beach cafés to sunbathers at their lounge chairs. It's often worth the euros to enjoy a private beach. If you see umbrellas on a beach, it means you'll have to pay a rental fee; otherwise the sand is free (all the beaches are marked on this book's Monterosso al Mare map). Prices get very soft in the afternoon. Don't use your white hotel towels; most hotels will give you beach towels—sometimes for a fee. The local hidden beach, which is free, gravelly, and generally less crowded, is tucked away under Il Casello restaurant at the east end of town, near the trailhead to Vernazza. There's another free beach at the far-west end, near the Gigante statue. The bocce ball court (next to Il Casello) is busy with the old boys enjoying their favorite pastime.

Kayaks

Samba rents kayaks on the beach (€7/hour for 1-person kayak, €12/hour for 2-person kayak, cheaper for longer rentals, to the right of train station as you exit, mobile 339-681-2265, Domenico). The paddle to Vernazza is a favorite. The adjacent **La Pineta** beach also rents stand-up paddleboards (€12/hour, Diego).

Shuttle Buses for High-Country Hikes

Monterosso's bus service (described earlier, under "Arrival in Monterosso") continues beyond the town limits, but check the schedules—only one or two departures a day head into the high country (and only in summer). Some buses go to the Sanctuary of Our Lady of Soviore, from where you can hike back down to Monterosso (1.5 hours, moderately steep). Rides cost €2.50 (free with Cinque Terre Park Card, pick up schedule from park office). Or you can hike to Levanto (no Cinque Terre Park card necessary, not as stunning as the rest of the coastal trail, 2.5 hours, straight uphill and then easy decline, follow signs at west end of the new town). For hiking details, ask at the train station TI.

Wine-Tasting

Buranco Agriturismo offers visits to their vineyard and cantina (reserve 2 days ahead). You'll taste two of their wines plus a grappa and a *limoncino,* along with home-cooked food (up to €25/person with snacks, English may be limited, follow Via Buranco uphill to path, 10 minutes above town, tel. 0187-817-677, www.burancocinqueterre.it). They also rent apartments; see "Sleeping in Monterosso," later.

Boat Rides

From the old town harbor, boats run nearly hourly (10:30-17:00) to Vernazza, Manarola, Riomaggiore, and Portovenere. Schedules are posted in Cinque Terre park offices.

Nightlife in Monterosso

Enoteca Eliseo, the first (and I'd say best) wine bar in town, comes with operatic ambience. Eliseo and his wife, Mary, love music and wine. You can select a fine bottle from their shop shelf, and for €7 extra, enjoy it and the village action from their cozy tables. If you've ever wanted an education in grappa, talk to Eliseo—he stocks more than a hundred varieties. Wines sold by the glass *(bicchiere)* are posted (Wed-Mon 14:00-24:00, closed Tue, Piazza Matteotti 3, a block inland behind church, tel. 0187-817-308).

Fast Bar, the best bar in town for young travelers and night owls, is located on Via Roma in the old town. Customers mix travel tales with big, cold beers, and the crowd (and the rock 'n' roll) gets noisier as the night rolls on. Come here to watch Italian or American sporting events on TV any time of day (€5 *panini* and €7-9 salads usually served until midnight, open Fri-Wed 9:30-2:00 in the morning, closed Thu except in peak season; Alex, Francisco, and Stefano).

La Cantina di Miky, in the new town just beyond the train station, is a trendy bar-restaurant with an extensive cocktail and grappa menu. The seating is in three zones: overlooking the beach, in the garden, or in the cellar. Run by Manuel, son of well-known local restaurateur Miky, it sometimes hosts live music. Manuel offers a fun "five villages" wine-tasting with local meats and cheeses (€15/person for just wine, €20/person with food). Microbrews are becoming popular in Italy, and this is the best place in town for top-end Italian beers (daily until well after 24:00, Via Fegina 90, tel. 0187-802-525).

Nuovo Eden Bar, overlooking the beach by the big rock just east of the train station, is a fine place to enjoy a cocktail or fancy ice cream with a sea view. During happy hour (16:30-21:00), €6 cocktails come with a snack. Locals consider their ice cream (either to-go from the streetside stand, or fancy and sit-down) the best in town. Consider this place for a pre-dinner drink or dessert with a view (Tue-Sun 7:30-24:00, closed Mon).

Sleeping in Monterosso

Monterosso, the most beach-resorty of the five Cinque Terre towns, offers maximum comfort and ease. The TI Proloco just outside the train station can give you a list of €70-80 double rooms. Rooms in Monterosso are a better value for your money than similar rooms in crowded Vernazza, and the proprietors seem more genuine and welcoming. To locate the hotels, see the Monterosso al Mare map.

In the Old Town

$$$ Hotel Villa Steno is lovingly managed and features great view balconies, panoramic gardens and a roof terrace with sun beds, air-conditioning, and the friendly help of English-speaking Matteo and his wife, Carla. Of their 16 rooms, 12 have view balconies (Sb-€115, Db-€180, Tb-€210, Qb-€260, includes hearty buffet breakfast, €10/night discount in 2014 when you pay cash and show this book, free guest computer and Wi-Fi, laundry, parking-€10—reserve in advance, hike up to the panoramic terrace, Via Roma 109, tel. 0187-817-028 or 0187-818-336, www.villasteno.com, steno@pasini.com). It's a 15-minute hike (or €8 taxi ride) from the train station to the top of the old town. Readers get a free Cinque Terre info packet and a glass of the local sweet wine, *Sciacchetrà,* when they check in—ask for it.

$$$ Albergo Pasquale is a modern, comfortable place with 15 rooms, run by the same family as the Hotel Villa Steno (above). It's conveniently located just a few steps from the beach, boat dock, tunnel entrance to the new town, and train tracks. While there is some train noise, the soundtrack is mostly a lullaby of waves. Located right on the harbor, it has an elevator and offers easier access than most (same prices and welcome drink as Villa Steno; all rooms with sea view, air-con, elevator, limited free Wi-Fi, Via Fegina 8, tel. 0187-817-550 or 0187-817-477, www.hotelpasquale. com, pasquale@pasini.com, Felicita and Marco).

$$$ Locanda il Maestrale rents six small, stylish rooms in a sophisticated and peaceful little inn. Although renovated with all the modern comforts, it retains centuries-old character under frescoed ceilings. Its peaceful sun terrace overlooking the old town and Via Roma action is a delight (small Db-€115, Db-€145, suite-€170, prices lower off-season, 10 percent Rick Steves discount if you book direct and pay cash, air-con, free Wi-Fi, Via Roma 37, tel. 0187-817-013, mobile 338-4530-531, www.locandamaestrale. net, maestrale@monterossonet.com, Stefania).

$$$ Il Giardino Incantato ("The Enchanted Garden") is a charming and comfortable four-room B&B with impressive atten- tion to detail in a tastefully renovated 16th-century Ligurian home in the heart of the old town. Breakfast is served under lemon trees in a delightful hidden garden, which is illuminated with candles in the evening (Db-€150-170, Db suite-€200, ask for Rick Steves discount, air-con, free Wi-Fi, free minibar and tea and coffee ser- vice, laundry service-€15/load, Via Mazzini 18, tel. 0187-818-315, mobile 333-264-9252, www.ilgiardinoincantato.net, giardino_in- cantato@libero.it, kind and eager-to-please Fausto and Mariapia).

$$$ L'Antica Terrazza rents four classy rooms right in town. With a pretty terrace overlooking the pedestrian street and minimal stairs, Raffaella and John offer a good deal (D with private bath down the hall-€85, Db-€115, these special prices for Rick Steves readers, 5 percent additional discount when you pay cash, air-con, free Wi-Fi, Vicolo San Martino 1, tel. 380-138-0082, mobile 347- 132-6213, www.anticaterrazza.com, post@anticaterrazza.com).

$$$ Albergo Marina, creatively run by enthusiastic husband- and-wife team Marina and Eraldo, has 23 decent rooms and a gar- den with lemon trees. With a free and filling buffet featuring local specialties from 14:00 to 17:00 daily, they offer a fine value (Db- €135, Tb-€160, Qb-€180, 10 percent discount in 2014 when you pay cash and show this book, elevator, air-con, pay Wi-Fi, free use of kayak and snorkel equipment, Via Buranco 40, tel. 0187-817-613, www.hotelmarina5terre.com, marina@hotelmarina5terre.com).

$$$ Hotel la Colonnina has 21 big and pretty rooms (some older, some newer), generous if dated public spaces, and several leafy, peaceful sun terraces. It's buried in the town's fragrant and sleepy back streets (Db-€143-153, Tb-€188, Qb-€233, €5 more for non-view mini-terrace, €15 more for townview terrace, cash only, air-con, free Wi-Fi, fridges, elevator, inviting rooftop terrace with sun beds, garden, in the old town a block inland from the main square at Via Zuecca 6, tel. 0187-817-439, www.lacolonninacinqueterre.it, info@lacolonninacinqueterre.it, Christina).

$$$ Manuel's Guesthouse, perched high above the town among terraces, is a garden getaway run by Lorenzo and his father, Giovanni (and named for their uncle/brother, a disheveled artist who prefers to set up his easels down below these days). They have six big, bright rooms and a grand view. After climbing the killer stairs from the town center, their killer terrace is hard to leave—especially after a few drinks (Db-€110, big Db with grand-view balcony-€130, cash only, air-con, free Wi-Fi, up about 100 steps behind church—you can ask Lorenzo to carry your bags up the hill, Via San Martino 39, mobile 333-439-0809, www.manuelsguesthouse.com, manuelsguesthouse@libero.it).

$$$ Buranco Agriturismo, a 10-minute hike above the old town, has wonderful gardens and views over the vine-covered valley. Its primary business is wine and olive-oil production, but they offer three apartments at a good price. It's a rare opportunity to stay in a farmhouse but still be able to get to town on foot (2-6 people-€60/person including breakfast, €30/child under 12, air-con, €7 taxi from station, tel. 0187-817-677, mobile 349-434-8046, www.burancocinqueterre.it, info@buranco.it, informally run by Loredana, Mary, and Giulietta).

$$ Albergo al Carugio is a simple, practical nine-room place in a big apartment-style building at the top of the old town. It's quiet, comfy, and functional (Db-€80, this price for Rick Steves readers when you book direct and pay cash, no breakfast, air-con, free Wi-Fi, Via Roma 100, tel. 0187-817-453, www.alcarugio.it, info@alcarugio.it, Andrea and Simona).

$ The Net Room Service is run by Enzo, who owns the Internet point in town (and speaks perfect English). He manages several apartments, offering Monterosso's least expensive accommodations. Enzo's office functions as your reception (Db-€60-70 any time of year, 2- or 3-night minimum stay, Via Vittorio Emanuele 55, tel. 0187-817-288, mobile 335-778-5085, www.monterossonet.com, info@monterossonet.com).

CINQUE TERRE

In the New Town

$$$ A Cà du Gigante, despite its name, is a tiny yet stylish refuge with nine rooms. About 100 yards from the beach (and surrounded by blocky apartments on a modern street), the interior is tastefully done with modern comfort in mind (Db-€160, Db seaview suite-€180, 10 percent discount with 3-night stay and this book in 2014, occasional last-minute deals, air-con, free Wi-Fi, free parking, Via IV Novembre 11, tel. 0187-817-401, www.ilgigantecinqueterre.it, gigante@ilgigantecinqueterre.it, Claudia).

$$$ Hotel Villa Adriana is a big, modern, bright hotel on a church-owned estate set in a peaceful garden with a pool, free parking, and a no-stress style. They rent 54 rooms—some with terraces and/or sea views—at the same price as much simpler places on the water (Sb-€90, Db-€170, all with showers, air-con, elevator, free Wi-Fi, free loaner bikes, Via IV Novembre 23, tel. 0187-818-109, www.villaadriana.info, info@villaadriana.info).

$$$ Hotel la Spiaggia is a venerable old 19-room place facing the beach and run with attitude by Andrea Poggi and his gentle daughter Maria. Half of the rooms come with air-con and half with sea views, but all are the same price—request what you like when you reserve (Db-€170, extra bed-€30, free parking, cash only, elevator, free Wi-Fi with this book, Via Lungomare 98, tel. 0187-817-567, www.laspiaggiahotel.com, hotellaspiaggia@libero.it).

$$$ Hotel Punta Mesco is a tidy, well-run little haven renting 17 quiet, modern rooms. While none have views, 10 rooms have small terraces. For the price, it may offer the best comfort in town (Db-€143, Tb-€185, 5 percent discount when you pay cash, air-con, free Wi-Fi, free parking, Via Molinelli 35, tel. 0187-817-495, www.hotelpuntamesco.it, info@hotelpuntamesco.it, Diego, Karina, and Manuel).

$$$ Pensione Agavi has 10 spartan, bright, overpriced rooms, about half overlooking the beach near the big rock. This is not a place to party—it feels like an old hospital with narrow hallways (D-€80, Db-€110, Tb-€145, rooms without view can be a bit cheaper, 10 percent discount for 2 nights or more, breakfast-€5, cash only, refrigerators, turn left out of station to Fegina 30, tel. 0187-817-171, mobile 333-697-4071, hotel.agavi@libero.it, Hillary).

$$ Affittacamere Ristorante il Gabbiano is an old-school, family-run restaurant right on the beach, renting five quiet, air-conditioned rooms upstairs. Three rooms face the sea, with small balconies (Db-€100, the largest can be Tb-€130, Qb-€160), while two are at the back, facing a little garden (Db-€90). The Gabbiano family restaurant serves as your reception (cash only, air-con, Via Fegina 84, tel. 0187-817-578, lella-v71@hotmail.it).

$ Le Sirene/Raggi di Sole, with nine simple rooms in two humble buildings, is about the cheapest place in town. It's run from a hole-in-the-wall reception desk a block from the station, just off the water. I'd request the Le Sirene building, which doesn't have train noise and is a bit more spacious and airy than Raggi di Sole (Db-€90, third person-€45, fans, free Wi-Fi in Raggi di Sole only, Via Molinelli 10, mobile 393-935-7683, www.sirenerooms.com, sirenerooms@gmail.com, Ermanna).

Eating in Monterosso

With a Sea View

Of these seaview restaurants, the first two offer reasonable prices right on the old town beach, while the last is a romantic splurge higher up.

Ristorante Belvedere, big and sprawling, is *the* place for a good-value meal indoors or outdoors on the harborfront. Their *amfora belvedere*—mixed seafood stew—is huge, and can easily be split among up to four diners (€48). Share with your group and add pasta for a fine meal. Mussel fans will enjoy the *tagliolini della casa* (€9). Their *misto mare* plate (2-person minimum, €15/person), a fishy treat, can nearly make an entire meal. It's energetically run by Federico and Roberto (€8-10 pastas, €10-16 *secondi*, Wed-Mon 12:00-14:30 & 18:00-22:00, usually closed Tue, on the harbor in the old town, tel. 0187-817-033).

Il Casello is the only place for a fun meal on a terrace overlooking the old town beach. With outdoor tables on a rocky outcrop, it's a pleasant spot for a salad, pasta, or *secondi* (€9-13 pastas, €13-18 *secondi*, daily April-Oct—food and drinks served all day long, closed Nov-March, mobile 333-492-7629, Bacco).

Ristorante Tortuga is the top option in Monterosso for seaview elegance, with gorgeous outdoor seating high on a bluff and an elegant white-tablecloth-and-candles interior. If you're looking for a place to propose, this offers the prettiest and most romantic dining in town. When you're out and about, drop by to consider which table you'd like to reserve for later. House specialties include *cannelloni tortuga* (stuffed not with turtle, but with sea bass) and *filetto Sciacchetrà*—steak with a glaze made of the local sweet wine (€15-19 pastas, €16-21 *secondi*, Tue-Sun 12:00-14:30 & 18:00-22:00, closed Mon, just outside the tunnel that connects the old and new town—or climb up the ramp in front of Albergo Pasquale, tel. 0187-800-065, mobile 333-240-7956, Silvia and Giamba).

In the Old Town

Via Venti is a quiet little trattoria, hidden in an alley deep in the heart of the old town, where Papa Ettore creates imaginative seafood dishes using the day's catch and freshly made pasta. Ilaria and her partner Michele serve up delicate and savory gnocchi (tiny potato dumplings) with crab sauce, tender ravioli stuffed with fresh fish, and pear-and-cheese pasta. There's nothing pretentious here... just good cooking, service, and prices (€11-13 pastas, €14-20 *secondi*, Fri-Wed 12:00-14:30 & 18:30-22:30, closed Thu, Via Venti 32, tel. 0187-818-347).

Ristorante al Pozzo is a favorite among locals. It's family-run, with good old-fashioned quality, as Gino (with his long white beard) cooks, and his engaging English-speaking son, Manuel, serves. They have one of the best wine lists in town, serve only homemade pasta, and are known for their raw fish and wonderful seafood *antipasti misti* (€10-17 pastas, €15-25 *secondi*, Fri-Wed 12:00-15:00 & 18:30-22:30, closed Thu, Via Roma 24, tel. 0187-817-575).

Ciak, high-energy and tightly packed, is a local institution with reliably good food and higher prices. It's known for its huge, sizzling terra-cotta crock for two crammed with the day's catch and accompanied by risotto or spaghetti, or served swimming in a soup *(zuppa)*. Other popular choices are fish ravioli with shrimp sauce and the seafood *antipasto Lampara* (€20). Stroll a couple of paces past the outdoor tables up Via Roma to see what Signore Ciak (who wears his Popeye cap in the kitchen) has on the stove (€13-14 pastas, €18-25 *secondi*, Thu-Tue 12:00-15:00 & 19:00-22:30, closed Wed, Via Roma 4, tel. 0187-817-014).

L'Alta Marea offers special fish ravioli, the catch of the day, and huge crocks of fresh, steamed mussels. Young chef Marco cooks with charisma, while his wife, Anna, takes good care of the guests. This place is quieter, buried in the old town two blocks off the beach, and has covered tables out front for people-watching (€9-13 pastas and pizza, €14-20 *secondi*, 10 percent discount with cash and this book, Thu-Tue 12:00-15:00 & 18:00-22:00, closed Wed, Via Roma 54, tel. 0187-817-170).

In the New Town

Even if you're not sleeping in the new town, consider venturing over for dinner at one of these options; as a bonus, the walk is mostly along a scenic and lively beachfront promenade.

Miky is packed with well-dressed locals who know their seafood and want to eat it in a classy environment. For elegantly presented, top-quality food, with subtle flavors that celebrate local ingredients and traditions, this is my Cinque Terre favorite. It's clearly a proud family operation: Miky (dad), Simonetta (mom), charming Sara (daughter, who greets guests), and the attentive but easygoing waitstaff all work hard. All their pasta is "pizza pasta"—cooked normally but finished in a bowl that's encased in a thin pizza crust. They cook the concoction in a wood-fired oven to keep in the aroma, then flambé it at your table. Miky's has a fine wine list with many available by the glass if you ask. If I were ever to require a dessert, it would be their mixed sampler plate, *dolce mista*—€10 and plenty for two (€15-18 pastas, €18-30 *secondi*, €8 sweets, Wed-Mon 12:00-15:00 & 19:00-23:00, closed Tue, reservations wise in summer, diners tend to dress up a bit—but it's not required, in the new town 100 yards north of train station at Via Fegina 104, tel. 0187-817-608).

La Cantina di Miky, a few doors down (toward the station), serves Ligurian specialties that follow in Miky's family tradition of quality. Run by son Manuel—and Christine from New Jersey—it's more trendy, youthful, and informal than Miky's. You can sit downstairs, in the garden, or overlooking the sea (€16 anchovy tasting plate, €10-13 pastas, €12-20 *secondi*, creative desserts, large selection of Italian microbrews, daily 12:00-24:00 or later, Via Fegina 90, tel. 0187-802-525). This place doubles as a cocktail bar in the evenings—see "Nightlife in Monterosso," earlier.

Light Meals, Take-Out Food, and Breakfast

In the Old Town: Lots of shops and bakeries sell pizza and focaccia for an easy picnic at the beach or on the trail. **Pizzeria la Smorfia**—the local favorite for pizza—cooks up good pizza to eat in or take out. Pizzas come in two sizes; the large can feed three (small pizzas-€6-9, large pizzas-€14-19, Fri-Wed 11:30-24:00, closed Thu, Via Vittorio Emanuele 73, tel. 0187-818-395). At **Il Frantoio,** Simone makes tasty pizza and focaccia to go or to munch perched on a stool (Fri-Wed 9:00-13:45 & 16:30-19:30, closed Thu, just off Via Roma at Via Gioberti 1). **Focacceria da Emy** (not to be confused with Pizzeria Ely, up the street) makes airy focaccia and thick-crust pizzas for casual seating or takeout (€5-7 pizza, €3 focaccia, daily 10:30-20:00, until 24:00 in summer, along the skinny street next to the church, Emigliano).

In the New Town, near the Station: For a quick bite right at the train station (or on the beach), consider **Il Massimo della Focaccia.** Massimo and Daniella serve local quiche-like tortes, sandwiches, focaccia pizzas, and desserts. With benches just in front, this is a good bet for a €4 light meal with a sea view (Thu-Tue 9:00-19:00, closed Wed, Via Fegina 50 at the entry to the station).

Breakfast: Most hotels include breakfast in the room rate. But if you're out looking for breakfast, in the new town, consider **Bar Gio,** near the train station on the waterfront (continental breakfasts); in the old town, look for **Bar Davi,** under the arch on Via Roma in the old town (with an American-style option, daily from 7:00).

Cinque Terre Connections

By Train

The five towns of the Cinque Terre are on a pokey milk-run train line. Erratically timed but roughly hourly trains connect each town with the others, plus La Spezia, Genoa, and Riviera towns to the north. While a few of these local trains go to more distant points (Milan or Pisa), it's much faster to change in La Spezia, Monterosso, or Sestri Levante to a bigger train (local train info tel. 0187-817-458, www.trenitalia.com).

From La Spezia Centrale by Train to: Rome (7/day, 3-4.5 hours, more with changes, €45; an evening train—departing around 20:00—gives you a complete day in the region while still getting you to Rome that night), **Pisa** (about hourly, 1-1.5 hours, €5), **Florence** (5/day direct, otherwise nearly hourly, 2.5 hours, €11.30), **Milan** (about hourly, 3 hours direct or with change in Genoa, €22), **Venice** (about hourly, 5-6 hours, 1-3 changes, €50).

From Monterosso by Train to: Venice (about hourly, 6-7 hours, 1-3 changes, €52), **Milan** (8/day direct, otherwise hourly with change in Genoa, 3-4 hours, €22), **Genoa** (hourly, 1.2-2 hours, €8), **Turin** (8/day, 3-4 hours, €20), **Pisa** (hourly, 1-2 hours, €6-10), **Sestri Levante** (hourly, 20-40 minutes, most trains to Genoa stop here, €3), **La Spezia** (2-3/hour, 15-30 minutes), **Levanto** (2-3/hour, 4 minutes), **Santa Margherita Ligure** (at least hourly, 45 minutes, €4.50), **Rome** (hourly, 4.5 hours, change in La Spezia, €50). For destinations in **France,** change trains in Genoa.

By Car

Because these towns are close together and have frequent transportation connections, bringing a car to the Cinque Terre is not the best idea. If your plans require it, however, here are some basic tips: Stay in a hotel that includes parking, use public transportation or hike between towns, and for day-trip parking, go to Monterosso (€14-18/day), Riomaggiore (€22/day), or Manarola (€15/day). Don't drive to Vernazza, as the flood blew out its main parking lot. Even if it's rebuilt, finding a spot will likely be tough. Parking anywhere on the Cinque Terre is truly a mess in July and August.

Milan to the Cinque Terre (130 miles): Drivers speed south on autostrada A-7 from Milan, skirt Genoa, and drive a little bit of Italy's curviest and narrowest freeways, passing the Cinque Terre toward the port of La Spezia (A-12). Another option is to take the slightly straighter A-1 via the city of Parma, followed by A-15 to La Spezia. This route takes the same amount of time (about 2.5 hours), even though it covers more miles.

The route from autostrada A-12 depends partly on the status of repairs to the 2011 flood damage. As of this writing (mid-2013), this is the best approach, but confirm details locally:

To reach **Monterosso** (about 30 minutes from the auto-strada), exit A-12 at *uscita Carrodano-Levanto*, northwest of La Spezia. Remember that the highway divides as you approach Monterosso—you must choose between the road to *Centro Storico* (the old town) or the one to *Fegina* (the new town and beachfront parking). Keep in mind that because of road closures (as of mid-2013), you can't reach Monterosso from La Spezia via the other Cinque Terre towns; you'll have to loop up to the SP-1/SP-38 highway.

For **Vernazza, Riomaggiore, Corniglia,** or **Manarola,** leave the freeway at La Spezia and follow the road that paral-lels the coast (with access to each of these four towns). The drive down to Vernazza is scenic, narrow, and scary; it's much bet-ter to park in La Spezia and ride the train in. While there is a secondary road connecting Vernazza and Monterosso, it's likely closed and—even if open—it's not recommended (the main road, SP-63, was washed out by the flood and will likely remain closed indefinitely—ask locally).

Within the Cinque Terre: On busy weekends, holidays, and in June, July, and August, both Vernazza and Monterosso fill up, and police at the top of town will deny entry to anyone without a hotel reservation. It's smart to have a confirmation in hand. If you don't, insist (politely) that they allow you to enter—but only if you actually have a room reserved (the police might call your hotel to check your story).

Parking Tips: Riomaggiore, Manarola, and Monterosso each have a parking lot and an hourly shuttle bus to get you into town, though all parking areas are no more than a 10-minute walk uphill from the center.

Blue signs post valid hours for pay parking, which usually don't charge from 24:00 to 8:00 (but read the signs or ask locals to be sure). Anyone can park where there are white lines. Park-ing is cash only in all towns (except Riomaggiore, where some readers have been overcharged on their credit cards—best to pay in cash).

If you plan to find parking in any of the Cinque Terre towns, try to arrive between 9:00 and 11:00, when overnight visitors are usually departing. Or you can park your car in Le-vanto or La Spezia, then take the train into the town of your choice. In these bigger towns, confirm that your parking spot is OK, and leave nothing inside to steal.

A few hotels offer parking for free or a daily charge. In **Mon-terosso,** consider Hotel Villa Steno, A Cà du Gigante, Hotel la

Spiaggia, or Hotel Punta Mesco. For **Riomaggiore,** try Locanda del Sole, Locanda Ca' dei Duxi, or Villa Argentina. In Volastra (a shuttle ride above **Manarola**), try Hotel il Saraceno. In **Corniglia,** try Il Carugio. Rooms listed in this book for Vernazza do not offer parking.

RIVIERA TOWNS NEAR THE CINQUE TERRE

Levanto • Sestri Levante • Santa Margherita Ligure • Portofino • La Spezia • Carrara • Portovenere

The Cinque Terre is tops, but several towns to the north have a breezy beauty and more beaches. Towns to the south offer a mix of marble, trains, and yachts.

Levanto, the northern gateway to the Cinque Terre, has a long beach and a scenic, strenuous trail to Monterosso al Mare. Sestri Levante, on a narrow peninsula flanked by two beaches, is for sunseekers. Santa Margherita Ligure is more of a real town, with actual sights, beaches, and easy connections with Portofino by trail, bus, or boat. All three towns are a straight shot to the Cinque Terre by train.

South of the Cinque Terre, you'll likely pass through the workaday town of La Spezia (don't stay here unless you're desperate), the southern gateway to the Cinque Terre. Carrara is a quickie for marble lovers who are driving between Pisa and La Spezia. The picturesque village of Portovenere, near La Spezia, has scenic boat connections with Cinque Terre towns.

Public transportation is the best way to get around this region. All the places in this chapter are well connected by train and/or boat.

North of the Cinque Terre

Levanto

Graced with a long, sandy beach, Levanto is packed in summer and popular with surfers. The rest of the year, it's just a small, sleepy town, with less charm and fewer tourists than the Cinque Terre. But with quick connections to Monterosso (4 minutes by train) and better dining options, Levanto makes a decent home base if you can't snare a room in the Cinque Terre.

Levanto has a new section (with a regular grid street plan) and a twisty old town (bisected by a modern street), plus a few pedestrian streets and a castle (not tourable). From Levanto, you can take a no-wimps-allowed hike to Monterosso (2.5 hours) or hop a boat to the Cinque Terre towns and beyond.

Orientation to Levanto

Tourist Information

The helpful TI is on Piazza Mazzini (daily 9:00-13:00 & 15:00-19:00 except Sun until 18:00, tel. 0187-808-125, www.comune.levanto.sp.it). The TI leads a weekly walking tour of Levanto's medieval architecture (free but tips expected, 2 hours, departs Tue at 18:00 from Piazza Cavour, register at TI).

Arrival in Levanto

By Train: It's a 10-minute walk from the Levanto train station to the TI in town (head down stairs in front of station, turn right, cross bridge, then follow Corso Roma to Piazza Mazzini).

By Car: Drivers can use the cheap **short-term parking** in the lots in front of and on either side of the train station (€7.20/8 hours, €10.80/24 hours—pay at machines each day). Another option is the lot across the river from the hospital on the way into town (first left after the hospital, cross bridge and immediately turn left), or north of the church on Via del Mercato (free during high season, except Wed before 14:00). For **long-term parking,** try the lots at Piazza Mazzini or behind the TI (€18/day).

Helpful Hints

Markets: Levanto's modern covered *mercato*, which sells produce and fish, is on Via del Mercato, between the TI and train station (Mon-Sat 8:00-13:00, closed Sun). On Wednesday

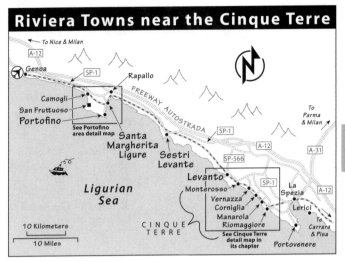

Riviera Towns near the Cinque Terre

morning, an **open-air market** with clothes, shoes, and house-
wares fills the street in front of the *mercato*.

Internet Access: Try **Viaggi Beraldi** at Via Garibaldi 102 (€2/30
minutes, Mon-Sat 9:00-12:30 & 15:30-19:30, closed Sun, tel.
0187-800-818).

Baggage Storage: None is available. Try La Spezia, Monterosso, or
Santa Margherita Ligure.

Laundry: A **self-service launderette** stuffed with snack and drink
vending machines is at Piazza Staglieno 38 (wash-€5 including soap, dry-€5, open 24 hours daily, mobile 338-701-6341).
Another self-service place, **Speedy Wash,** is at Via Garibaldi
32 (wash-€4, dry-€2, daily 8:00-21:00, mobile 350-156-5026).

Bike Rental: Cicli Raso North Shore rents bikes (€10-20/day
depending on type of bike, daily 9:30-12:30 & 15:30-19:30,
closed Sun Nov-April, Via Garibaldi 63, tel. 0187-802-511,
www.cicliraso.com). The **Sensafreni Bike Shop** is convenient
to the beach boardwalk (€2/hour, €15/24 hours, Mon-Sat
9:30-12:30 & 16:00-19:30, closed Sun, Piazza del Popolo 1,
tel. 0187-807-128).

Sports Rentals: Rosa dei Venti rents kayaks, canoes, surfboards,
and windsurfing equipment right on the beach (Marco mobile
329-451-1981, www.levantorosadeiventi.it).

Sights in Levanto

Beach

You can access Levanto's beach boardwalk and the sea right behind
the TI. As you face the harbor, the boat dock is to your far left, and

Levanto

1. Albergo Primavera
2. Villa Margherita
3. Garden Hotel
4. To Hotels Carla & Dora
5. A Durmì Guesthouse
6. Ristorante la Loggia Rooms
7. Villa Clelia B&B
8. La Rosa dei Venti Rooms
9. Agriturismo A Due Passi dal Mare
10. To Erba Persa Agriturismo
11. Ostello Ospitalia del Mare
12. Osteria Tumelin
13. Da Rino Trattoria
14. Ristorante Moresco
15. Taverna Garibaldi & Bike Rental
16. La Picea Pizzeria
17. Focacceria il Falcone
18. Il Laboratorio del Pesto
19. Dimarket Supermarket
20. Crai Supermarkets (2)
21. Il Pinguino Gelateria
22. Il Porticciolo Gelateria
23. Internet Café
24. Launderettes (2)
25. Canoe & Kayak Rental
26. Bike Rental

RIVIERA TOWNS

the diving center is to your far right (rental boats available at either place in summer). You can also rent a kayak or canoe on the beach, just below the east end of the Piazza Mazzini parking lot.

During the summer, three parts of the beach are free: both sides of the boat dock, and behind the TI. The rest of the beach is broken up into private sections that charge admission. You can always stroll along the beach, even through the private sections—

just don't sit down. Off-season, roughly October through May, the entire beach is free, and you can lay your towel anywhere you like.

Old Town and Trailhead
The old town, several blocks from the TI and beach, clusters around Piazza del Popolo. Until a few decades ago, the town's open-air market was held at the 13th-century loggia (covered set of archways) in the square. Explore the back streets.

To reach the trailhead to Monterosso: From Piazza del Popolo, head uphill to the striped church, Chiesa di Sant'Andrea (with your back to the loggia, go straight ahead—across the square and up Via Don Emanuele Toso to the church). From the church courtyard, follow the sign to the *castello* (a private residence), go under the stone arch, and continue uphill. Or, if you're coming from the seaside promenade (Via Gaetano Semenza), head under the arches and up the stairs, and follow the signs to the *castello*. Either route leads you to a sign that points you toward Punta Mesco, the rugged tip of the peninsula. From here, you can hike up to Monterosso (2.5 hours). This lovely, rugged-and-wild hike is no joke—bring lots of water and wear good shoes. Most of the trail is a gradual up-and-down, but the last stretch into Monterosso is almost entirely big steps, so those with knee problems might consider starting in Monterosso instead. The elevation gain overall is more than double that of the toughest Cinque Terre hikes. The Cinque Terre hiking pass is not necessary here.

Hike or Bike to Bonassola and Beyond
Cross the river bridge located by the TI to wander along this easy waterfront path, good for walking or cycling. You'll encounter shaded tunnels and two sunny beaches on the way to the small but modern town of Bonassola with its sandy beach (25 minutes by foot, 10 minutes by bike, public beaches located a minute's walk down from trail). From Bonassola, the path continues on to the town of Framura, a 3.5-mile walk/ride from Levanto.

Sleeping in Levanto

In this popular beach town, many hotels want you to take half-pension (lunch or dinner) in summer, especially in July and August. Prices listed here are the maximum for high season (July-Aug); smaller rooms or those without views may be less. Expect to pay €10-30 less per night for April-June and September-October, and even less for the rest of the year. The longer your stay, the greater your bargaining power. The high number of four-person rooms in Levanto makes it particularly welcoming to families who want to explore the Cinque Terre. Many hotels rent out large apartments with kitchenettes (without a half-pension requirement), and parking is free or very reasonable.

Sleep Code

(€1 = about $1.30, country code: 39)
S = Single, **D** = Double/Twin, **T** = Triple, **Q** = Quad, **b** = bathroom, **s** = shower only. Unless otherwise noted, credit cards are accepted, English is spoken, and breakfast is included. Many cities in Italy levy a hotel tax of €2 per person, per night, which must be paid in cash (not included in the rates I've quoted).

To help you sort easily through these listings, I've divided the accommodations into three categories based on the price for a standard double room with bath:

$$$ Higher Priced—Most rooms €110 or more.
$$ Moderately Priced—Most rooms between €50-110.
$ Lower Priced—Most rooms €50 or less.

Prices can change without notice; verify the hotel's current rates online or by email. For the best prices, always book direct.

$$$ Albergo Primavera is family-run, with 17 redecorated, tasteful rooms—10 with balconies but no views—just a half-block from the beach (Db-€140 if you book directly with the hotel, request a quiet room off the street, includes hearty breakfast buffet with local hams and cheeses, air-con, guest computer, Wi-Fi, free loaner bikes, Via Cairoli 5, tel. 0187-808-023, www.primaverahotel.com, info@primaverahotel.com, friendly Carlo, cheerful Daniela, and daughters Giuditta and Gloria). Carlo can arrange airport transfers on request.

$$$ Villa Margherita is 300 yards out of town, but the shady gardens, 11 characteristic colorfully tiled rooms (some with little view terraces), and tranquility are worth the walk (Db-€170, Tb-€185, 5 percent discount with cash and this book, elevator one flight up from street level, guest computer, free Wi-Fi, free parking, 10-minute walk to town with stairs, 5-minute walk to train station, free shuttle service from station if you tell them when you'll arrive, Via Trento e Trieste 31, tel. 0187-807-212, mobile 328-842-6934, www.villamargherita.net, info@villamargherita.net). They also rent apartments around town and a fancy villa (for up to 14 people) set on a peninsula by the sea (www.levanto.net).

$$$ Garden Hotel offers 17 simple, bright, modern rooms, all with balconies (but most lack views due to the elevated street), a block from the beach on busy Corso Italia (Db-€120, newer fifth-floor room with sea views and terrace-Db-€148, 5 percent discount with cash and this book, closed mid-Nov-mid-March, air-con, elevator for fifth floor only, free Wi-Fi, free parking but not on-site—can unload bags and then park near the station, loaner bikes, Corso Italia 6, tel. 0187-808-173, www.nuovogarden.com, info@ nuovogarden.com, Davide and Damiano).

$$$ Hotel Carla's 30 brand-new rooms are decorated in soothing, modish colors. It's located just five minutes from the station and 10 minutes from the beach (Db-€85-140, Via Martiri della Libertà 28, tel. 0187-808-275, www.carlahotel.com, info@ carlahotel.com).

$$ A Durmì is a happy little *affitta camere* (guesthouse) owned by lovely Graziella, Gianni, and their two daughters, Elisa and Chiara. Their sunny patios, green leafy gardens, six immaculate modern new rooms, and five sunlit apartments make a welcoming place to stay (Db-€60-110, extra bed-€20; 3-4 person apartment-€90-160—no minimum stay required; ask about cash discount when you book, rooms cleaned daily, breakfast-€7, air-con, power showers, guest computer, Wi-Fi in lobby, bar, parking-€5/ day, Via D. Viviani 12, tel. 0187-800-823, mobile 349-105-6016, www.adurmi.it, info@adurmi.it).

$$ Ristorante la Loggia has four pleasant, cozy, summery rooms perched above the old loggia on Piazza del Popolo (Db-€70, cash only, request balcony, quieter rooms in back, two basic side-by-side apartments great for families of 4-8, lots of stairs, air-con, free parking, Piazza del Popolo 7, tel. & fax 0187-808-107, mobile 335-641-7701, www.loggialevanto.com, Nerina does not speak English).

$$ Villa Clelia B&B offers six peaceful, dark, air-conditioned rooms (named for the winds—*scirocco, maestrale,* and so on) with mini-fridges and terraces in a garden courtyard just 50 yards from the sea (Db-€75-95, minimal in-room breakfast, Wi-Fi, free parking; with loggia on your left, it's straight ahead at Piazza da Passano 1; tel. 0187-808-195, mobile 329-379-4859, www.villaclelia. it, info@villaclelia.it). They also have seven central apartments that economically sleep up to five (€800/week, 3-night minimum stay). B&B rooms are cleaned daily; you're on your own at the apartments.

$$ La Rosa dei Venti is an *affitta camere* just a couple of blocks from the beach. Enthusiastic Rosanna and her son Marco rent five super-clean rooms with dark hardwood floors, comfy rugs, and a hodgepodge of glittery seashore decor (Db-€110, Tb-€135, includes homemade breakfast, air-con, free Wi-Fi, free parking, behind Enoteca Tumelin across from Piazza del Popolo, Via della Compera, tel. 0187-808-165, Marco's mobile 328-742-8268, www. larosadeiventilevanto.com, info@larosadeiventilevanto.com).

$$ Agriturismo A Due Passi dal Mare is an in-town oasis, just a five-minute walk from the beach or the train station. Friendly Francesca and husband Maurizio rent four crisp, quiet rooms with sizeable bathrooms; their back garden is open to guests (Sb-€50, Db-€80, Tb-€100, cheaper in spring and fall, free Wi-Fi and on-site parking, closed Jan-Feb, right on the main drag at Corso Roma 37, tel. 0187-809-177, mobile 338-960-1537, www.a2passidalmare.com, info@a2passidalmare.com).

$$ Hotel Dora has perfectly comfortable (if dated) rooms in a quiet residential neighborhood a 10-minute walk from the beach (Db-€100-120, Via Martiri della Libertà 27, tel. 0187-808-168, www.dorahotel.it, info@dorahotel.it).

$$ Erba Persa Agriturismo, a rustic farmhouse run by sunny Grazia Lizza and her gardener husband Claudio, hosts cats, dogs, pet rabbits, and donkeys among their plots of organic fruits and vegetables. The three rooms are old-fashioned but roomy. It's a 10-minute walk from the train station and about a 20-minute walk from town (D-€50, Db with balcony and countryside view-€70, extra bed-€10, free Wi-Fi, free parking, free mosquitoes, Via N. S. della Guardia 21, mobile 339-400-8587 or 348-344-7695, www.erbapersa.it, erbapersa@alice.it).

Hostel: **$ Ostello Ospitalia del Mare,** a budget gem, is run by the city tourist association. It has 70 basic beds, airy rooms, an elevator, and a terrace in a well-renovated medieval palazzo a few steps from the old town (beds-€19-27 in 4-, 6-, and 8-bed rooms with private bath, Db-€65; includes breakfast, thin towels, and sheets; guest computer, free Wi-Fi, self-service laundry-€7.50, microwave, fridge, nonmembers welcome, co-ed unless you strenuously object, no curfew, no lockout; office open daily April-Oct 8:00-13:00 & 16:00-20:00, until 23:00 weekend nights, slightly shorter hours off-season; may close Nov-March, Via San Nicolò 1, tel. 0187-802-562, www.ospitaliadelmare.it, info@ospitaliadelmare.it).

Eating in Levanto

Osteria Tumelin, a local favorite, is more expensive than other options, but has a dressy, sophisticated ambience and a wide selection of fresh seafood. Reservations are smart on weekends or if you want to dine outside (€12-14 *primi*, €17-23 *secondi*, daily 12:00-14:30 & 19:00-22:30, closed Thu Oct-May, aquarium containing giant lobster and moray eels in first dining room on the right, Via D. Grillo 32, across street from loggia, tel. 0187-808-379).

Da Rino, a small trattoria on a quiet pedestrian lane, dishes up reasonably priced fresh seafood and homemade Ligurian specialties prepared with care. Consider the grilled *totani* (squid), *pansotti con salsa di noci* (ravioli with walnut sauce), and *trofie al pesto* (local pasta with pesto sauce). Dine indoors or at one of the outdoor tables. On busy nights, they open up a second dining room across the street. Sommelier Anna will help you choose a good wine (€8-11 pastas, €13-15 *secondi,* daily 19:00-22:00, closed Tue, Via Garibaldi 10, tel. 0187-813-475).

Ristorante la Loggia, next to the old loggia, makes fine food, including gnocchi with scampi and saffron sauce and a delectable seafood lasagna. Their daily fish specials are served in a homey, wood-paneled dining room or on a little terrace overlooking the square (€10-12 pastas, €15-17 *secondi,* Thu-Tue 12:30-14:00 & 19:00-22:00, closed Wed, closed Nov-Feb, Piazza del Popolo 7, tel. 0187-808-107).

Ristorante Moresco serves large portions of pasta and seafood at reasonable prices in a vaulted, candlelit room decorated with Moorish-style frescoes. The best value is their €25 four-course tasting *menu* (doesn't include drinks, 2-person minimum). Skip the house white wine and order something more drinkable from their wine list (daily 12:00-14:00 & 19:00-20:00—or until the last diner leaves, may close Sun evenings in winter, reservations appreciated, Via Jacopo 24, tel. 0187-807-253, busy Roberto and Francesca).

Taverna Garibaldi is a good-value, cozy place on the most characteristic street in Levanto, serving focaccia with various toppings, made-to-order *farinata* (savory chickpea crêpe), 34 types of pizza, and salads (€8-10 light meals, daily in summer 19:00-22:00, likely closed Tue Sept-June, Via Garibaldi 57, tel. 0187-808-098).

La Picea serves up wood-fired pizzas to go, or dine at one of their few small tables (Tue-Sun 16:30-21:45, closed Mon, just off the corner near Via Varego at Via della Concia 18, tel. 0187-802-063).

A Picnic or Bite on the Go: Focaccerie, rosticcerie, and delis with take-out pasta abound on Via Dante Alighieri. **Focacceria il Falcone** has a great selection of focaccia with different toppings (daily 9:30-22:00, Oct-May closes at 20:00 and on Mon, Via Cairoli 19, tel. 0187-807-370). For more picnic options, try the *mercato* (mornings except Sun). It's fun to grab a crusty loaf of bread, then pair it with a pot of freshly made Genovese pesto from **Il Laboratorio del Pesto** (sometimes closed Wed afternoons, Via Dante 14, tel. 0187-807-441). The **Dimarket supermarket** just below the train station has a good deli counter and opens at 7:00—handy for those taking an early train. There are two **Crai supermarkets.** One is just off Via Jacopo da Levanto at Via del Municipio 5 (Mon-Sat 8:00-13:00 & 17:00-20:00, Sun 8:00-13:00 & 16:30-19:30); the other is nearby on Piazza Staglieno (for a shaded setting, lay out your spread on a bench in the grassy park at this piazza). Another excellent picnic spot is Piazza Cristoforo Colombo, located east of the swimming pool, with benches and sea views.

And for Dessert: Compare **Il Pinguino Gelateria** at Piazza

Staglieno 2 (daily until late) with **Il Porticciolo Gelateria,** at the end of Via Cairoli at Piazzetta Marina (daily in summer, closed Mon Sept-June, mobile 393-228-1570).

Levanto Connections

From Levanto: To get to the Cinque Terre, you can take the **train** (2-3/hour, 4 minutes to Monterosso). A slower, more scenic option is the **boat,** which stops at every Cinque Terre town—except Corniglia—before heading to Portovenere (2/day Easter-Oct, none Nov-Easter; €7 one-way to Monterosso, 10:00 departure includes Cinque Terre, Portovenere, and Lerici Island tour for €28; 14:30 departure includes Cinque Terre and 1-hour stop in Portovenere for €18; 1 return boat each day from Portovenere departs at about 17:00; pick up boat schedule and price sheet from TI or boat dock, tel. 0187-732-987 or on weekends 0187-777-727, www.navigazionegolfodeipoeti.it).

Sestri Levante

This peninsular town is squeezed as skinny as a hot dog between its two beaches. The pedestrian-friendly Corso Colombo, which runs down the middle of the peninsula, is lined with shops that sell take-away pizza, pastries, and beach paraphernalia. Don't be discouraged by the ugly modern town in front of the train station; the peninsula, about a seven-minute walk away, has charm to spare.

Hans Christian Andersen enjoyed his visit here in the mid-1800s, writing, "What a fabulous evening I spent in Sestri Levante!" One of the bays—Baia delle Favole—is named in his honor (*favole* means "fairy tale"). The small mermaid curled on the edge of the fountain behind the TI is another nod to the beloved Danish storyteller.

During the last week of May, the town awards its Hans Christian Andersen Prize, created to celebrate children's literature. Open to professional writers worldwide as well as school children throughout Italy, the competition culminates in a street festival and an awards ceremony for the best fairy tale in four age groups. The "Oscars" are little mermaids.

Orientation to Sestri Levante

Tourist Information: From the train station, it's a five-minute walk to the TI, where you can pick up a map (Tue-Sat 9:30-13:00 & 14:00-17:30, closed Sun-Mon; go straight out of station on Via

Roma, turn left at fountain in park, TI in next square at Piazza Sant'Antonio 10; tel. 0185-457-011). They can also direct you to the trail (south of town) for a one-hour hike to the scenic Punta Manara promontory.

Market Day: It's on Saturday at Piazza Aldo Moro (8:00-13:00). Local producers of olive oil, cheese, jam, and honey also set up on occasional Sundays on Via Asilo Maria Teresa (where Via XXV Aprile and Corso Columbo meet).

Baggage Storage: None is available at the station.

Laundry: There's a self-service launderette not far from the train station (wash-€5, daily 8:30-20:30, Via Costantino Raffo 8, mobile 329-012-8885).

Sights in Sestri Levante

Stroll the Town

From the TI, take Corso Colombo (to the left of Bermuda Bar, eventually turns into Via XXV Aprile, then Via alla Penisola), which runs up the peninsula. Follow this street—lively with shops, eateries, and delightful pastel facades—for about five minutes. Just before you get to Piazza Matteotti with the large white church at the end, turn off for either beach (free Silenzio beach is on your left). Or continue on the street to the left of the church and head uphill. You'll pass the evocative arches of a ruined chapel (bombed during World War II and left as a memorial). A few minutes farther on, past a stony Romanesque church, the road winds to the right to the Grand Hotel dei Castelli. Consider a drink at their view café (so-so view, reasonably priced drinks, daily 10:00-24:00, café entrance is at end of parking lot). The rocky, forested bluff at the end of the town's peninsula is actually the huge private backyard of this fancy hotel.

Beaches

These are named after the bays *(baie)* that they border. The bigger beach, Baia delle Favole, is divided up much of the year (May-Sept) into sections that you must pay to enter. The fees, which can soar up to €30 per day in August (no hourly rate), generally include chairs, umbrellas, and fewer crowds. There are several small free sections: at the ends and in the middle (look for *libere* signs, and ask *"Gratis?"* to make sure that it's free). For less expensive sections of beach (where you can rent a chair for about €8-10), ask for *spiaggia libera attrezzata* (spee-AH-jah LEE-behr-ah ah-treh-ZAHT-tah). The usual beach-town activities are clustered along this *baia:* boat rentals, sailing lessons, and bocce courts—ask if you can get in on a game.

The town's other beach, Baia del Silenzio, is narrow, virtually all free, and packed, providing a good chance to see Italian

Sestri Levante

1. Hotel Due Mari
2. Hotel Helvetia
3. Hotel Celeste
4. Hotel Mira
5. Hotel Genova
6. Albergo Marina
7. Villa Jolanda
8. L'Osteria Mattana
9. Polpo Mario, Ristorante Mainolla & Minimarket Fabrizio
10. Bacciolo Gelato
11. Ice Cream's Angels
12. Supermarkets (2)
13. Rosticceria Bertolone

families at play. There isn't much more to do here than unroll a beach towel and join in. At the far end of Baia del Silenzio (under Hotel Helvetia) is Citto Beach bar, which offers front-row seats with bay views (drinks daily June-Aug 10:00-24:00, May and Sept-Oct until 20:00, sandwiches and salads at lunchtime only, closed Nov-April, Gilberto).

Sleeping in Sestri Levante

Prices listed here are the maximum for the high season (July-Aug). Prices are €10-20 less per night April-June and September-October, and soft the rest of the year. Some hotels are closed off-season.

$$$ Hotel Due Mari, located in an old Genoese palazzo with sprawling public spaces, has three stars, 65 fine rooms, and a rooftop terrace with a super view of both beaches. Ideally, reserve well in advance. The extra services and grand communal spaces are the draw (small Db-€110, bigger Db-€140-220 depending on view and type of room, €35/person half-pension in aristocratic restaurant required July-Aug, closed mid-Oct-Dec, air-con, guest computer, Wi-Fi, elevator, garden, outdoor and heated indoor seawater swimming pools, wet sauna, small gym, parking-€15/day; take Corso Colombo to the end, hotel is behind church in Piazza Matteotti—take the left-hand alleyway flanking church, Vico del Coro 18; tel. 0185-42695, www.duemarihotel.it, info@duemarihotel.it).

$$$ Hotel Helvetia, overlooking Baia del Silenzio, feels posh and romantic, with 21 bright rooms, a large sun terrace with a heated, cliff-hanging swimming pool, and a peaceful garden atmosphere (viewless Db-€210-230, Db with sea view/balcony-€250-280, closed Nov-March, air-con, elevator, free Wi-Fi, swimming pool, off-site parking-€15/day with free shuttle; from Corso Colombo, turn left on Via Palestro and angle left at the small square to Via Cappuccini 43, tel. 0185-41175, www.hotelhelvetia.it, helvetia@hotelhelvetia.it, Alex).

$$$ Hotel Celeste, a dream for beach lovers, rests along the waterfront. Its 41 rooms are modern and plainly outfitted—you pay for the sea breeze (Db-€165 with view and balcony, €25 optional half-pension, air-con, elevator, guest computer, free Wi-Fi, deals on beach chairs, attached beachside bar, Lungomare Descalzo 14, tel. 0185-485-005, www.hotelceleste.com, info@hotelceleste.com, Franco).

$$$ Hotel Mira is an old-school hotel on the beachfront promenade, just around the corner from the town's charming historical core and handy to the beaches. Rooms are simply furnished, yet have all amenities (Db-€150-160, Tb-€180-190, includes breakfast, Viale Rimembranza 15, tel. 0185-459-404, www.hotelmira.com, info@hotelmira.com).

$$$ Hotel Genova, run by the Bertoni family, is a ship-shape hotel with 27 shiny-clean, modern, and cheery rooms, sunny lounge, rooftop sundeck, free loaner bikes, and a good location just two blocks from Baia delle Favole (Sb-€75, Db-€130, superior Db-€150, Tb-€189, ask for quieter room in back, air-con, elevator, Wi-Fi, parking-€5/day; from the train station, walk straight ahead, turn right at the T-intersection, and find the cream building ahead on the right, Viale Mazzini 126; tel. 0185-41057, www.hotelgenovasestrilevante.com, info@hotelgenovasestrilevante.com, Stefano).

$$ Albergo Marina's friendly Magda and her brother Santo rent 23 bright, peaceful, and clean rooms done in sea-foam green. Though the hotel is located on a busy boulevard, all rooms are at the back, facing a quiet courtyard and parking lots, and priced right (Db-€65-85, half-pension optional, air-con, elevator, Wi-Fi in lobby, self-service laundry, pool table; exit the train station and angle left down Via Eraldo, at Piazza Repubblica, take an easy left onto Via Fasce and find the hotel ahead on the right, Via Fasce 100; tel. 0185-487-332, www.marinahotel.it, marinahotel@marinahotel.it).

$$ Villa Jolanda is a homey, kid-friendly, basic *pensione* with 17 simple rooms, five with little balconies but no views, new bathrooms, and a garden courtyard/sun terrace—perfect for families on a budget...and the owner's cats (Sb-€30-45, Db-€75-95, Qb-€100-120, 3-night minimum stay required with advance reservation, €6.50 breakfast isn't worth it but owner Mario's €23 home-cooked dinners are—available June-Aug only, free parking; located near Baia del Silenzio—take alley just to the right of the church on Piazza Matteotti, Via Pozzetto 15, tel. 0185-41354, www.villajolanda.it, info@villajolanda.it).

Eating in Sestri Levante

Everything I've listed is on classic Via XXV Aprile, which also abounds with *focaccerie,* take-out pizza by the slice, and little grocery shops. Assemble a picnic or try one of the places below.

At **L'Osteria Mattana,** where everyone shares long tables in two dining rooms (the second one is in the back, past the wood oven and brazier), you can mix with locals while enjoying traditional cuisine, listed on chalkboard menus. Handy translations are posted next to the boards (Mon-Fri 19:30-22:00, Sat-Sun 12:30-14:30 & 19:30-22:30, no dinner served Mon Nov-April, cash only; follow Corso Colombo from TI as it turns into Via XXV Aprile, restaurant on right at #36; tel. 0185-457-633, Marco).

Polpo Mario is classier but affordable, with a fun people-watching location on the main drag (€14-16 pastas, €18-22 *secondi,* €40 fixed-price tasting *menu,* Tue-Sun 12:15-15:00 & 19:00-23:00, closed Mon, Via XXV Aprile 163, tel. 0185-480-203).

Ristorante Mainolla offers €4-8 pizzas, big salads, focaccia sandwiches, and reasonably priced pastas near Baia del Silenzio (daily in summer 12:00-16:00 & 19:00-22:00, closed Tue off-season, Via XXV Aprile 187, mobile 338-157-0877).

Gelato: Locals flock to **Ice Cream's Angels** at the intersection of Via XXV Aprile and Via della Chiusa. Riccardo and Elena artfully load up your cone with intermingling flavors, and top it with a dollop of Nutella chocolate-hazelnut cream (open daily until late in summer, closed Tue off-season, mobile 348-402-1604). **Bacciolo** enjoys a similar popularity among residents (closed Thu, Via XXV Aprile 51, on the right just before the church).

Supermarket: You can stock up on picnic supplies at two locations of **Carrefour Express** on Piazza della Repubblica, at #1 (Mon-Sat 8:00-13:00 & 15:30-20:00, closed Sun) and #28 (daily 8:30-20:00). Or pop into the conveniently located **Minimarket Fabrizio** for fresh fruit, *salumi,* and bread (Thu-Tue 8:00-12:30 & 16:00-19:30, closed Wed and sometimes Sun, Via XXV Aprile 177).

Deli: For a take-out meal, head to **Rosticceria Bertolone** for roasted anything—beef, pork, chicken, or vegetables. Assemble an entire meal from their deli and ask them to heat it for you (Mon-Sat 7:30-13:00 & 16:00-19:30, closed Sun, Via Fasce 12, tel. 0185-487-098).

Sestri Levante Connections

By **train,** Sestri Levante is just 20-40 minutes away from Monterosso (hourly connections with Monterosso, nearly hourly with other Cinque Terre towns) and 30 minutes from Santa Margherita Ligure (2/hour).

Boats depart to the Cinque Terre, Santa Margherita Ligure, Portofino, and San Fruttuoso from the dock *(molo)* on the peninsula (boats run Easter-Oct; to get to the dock: facing the church in Piazza Matteotti, take the road on the right with the sea on your right, about halfway down Via Pilade Queirolo; tel. 0185-284-670, mobile 336-253-336, www.traghettiportofino.it).

Santa Margherita Ligure

If you need the Riviera of movie stars, park your yacht at Portofino. Or you can settle down with more elbow room in nearby and personable Santa Margherita Ligure (15 minutes by bus from

Portofino and one hour by train from the Cinque Terre). While Portofino's velour allure is tarnished by a nonstop traffic jam in peak season, Santa Margherita tumbles easily downhill from its train station. The town has a fun Old World resort character and a breezy harborfront.

On a quick day trip from Milan or the Cinque Terre, walk the beach promenade and see the small old town of Santa Margherita Ligure before catching the bus (or boat) to Portofino to see what all the fuss is about. With more time, Santa Margherita makes a fine overnight stop or home base for hiking the Portofino peninsula.

Orientation to
Santa Margherita Ligure

Tourist Information

Pick up a map at the harborside TI on Piazza Veneto (daily April-Sept 9:30-12:30 & 14:30-19:30, Oct-March closes at 17:30 and all day Sun, tel. 0185-287-485, www.turismoinliguria.it).

Arrival by Train

To get from the station to the city center, take the stairs marked *Mare* (sea) down to the harbor; for an easier descent (especially if you're wheeling a suitcase), head down the gentler grade of Via Roma (follow *TI* signs). The harborfront promenade is wider than the skimpy beach. (The real beaches, which are pebbly, are a 10-minute walk farther on, past the port.)

The TI is right on the waterfront at Piazza Veneto (with the roundabout, flags, and park). The pedestrian-friendly old town is a block away: From the piazza, head inland on Largo Antonio Giusti and take a near-immediate left onto Via Torino, which opens onto Piazza Caprera, a square with a church and morning fruit vendors in the midst of traffic-free streets.

Helpful Hints

Internet Access: Papiluc Bar has two terminals (€3/30 minutes, daily 6:30 until late, Via del Arco 20, tel. 0185-282-580).

Post Office: It's just down the road from the train station on Via Roma (Mon-Fri 8:20-19:05, Sat 8:20-12:35, closed Sun, Via Roma 36).

Baggage Storage: There's no official left-luggage office, but day-trippers arriving by train can stash their bags at the station's café-bar (next to the station).

Pharmacy: There's one at Via Roma, near the post office, and another at the corner of Piazza Caprera and Via Pescino, not far from the TI.

Bike Rental: GM Rent is at Via XXV Aprile 11 (€10/5 hours, €20/24 hours, also rents scooters and Smart Cars, daily 10:00-13:00 & 16:30-20:00, mobile 329-406-6274, www.gmrent.it, Francesco).

Taxi: Taxis wait outside the train station and charge €15 for a ride from the station to anywhere in town, €25 to Paraggi beach, and €35 to Portofino (tel. 0185-286-508).

Driver: Helpful taxi driver **Alessandro** is also available for airport transfers and local excursions (mobile 338-860-2349, www.alessandrotaxi.com, alessandrotaxi@yahoo.it).

Parking: The recommended **Hotel Mediterraneo** and **Villa Anita** offer free parking to their guests, and a few hotels have

Santa Margherita Ligure

100 Meters
100 Yards

TRAIN STATION

CORSO E. RAINUSSO ROMA

POST

RIVIERA TOWNS

VIA XXV APRILE

CORSO MATTEOTTI

VIA BOZZO

VIA

Piazza Mazz.

VIA BELVEDERE

PALESTRO

CAIROLI

SOLIMANO

GIUNCHETO

Largo Giusti

PIAZZA Caprera

Piazza Veneto

FREE BEACH

To Rapallo & Freeway

PAGANA

V. GRAMSCI

A. DORIA

VIA TRIESTE

VIA ZARA

ROMA

ARCO

BUS STOP TO PORTOFINO

Piazza della Libertà

VIRGIN MARTYR STATUE

BOAT DOCK

CASTLE

Ligurian Sea

SANTA MARGHERITA

VILLA DURAZZO

Durazzo Park

CAFE

SAN GIACOMO

SANT' ERASMO

FISH MARKET

Marina

S. GIACOMO

VIA FAVALE

VIA P. CENTURIONE

DOGALI

GORIZA

CORSO G. MARCONI

To Portofino, Paraggi Beach & ❺

❶ Hotel Jolanda
❷ Hotel Tigullio et de Milan
❸ Hotel Mediterraneo
❹ Hotel Laurin
❺ To Villa Anita, Rist. A' Lampara & Bar Giuli
❻ Hotel Nuova Riviera
❼ Hotel Fasce
❽ La Cambusa Ristorante
❾ Dal Baffo Ristorante
❿ Da Pezzi Ristorante
⓫ Da Gennaro Pizzeria
⓬ Simonetti Gelateria
⓭ Gelateria Centrale
⓮ Seghezzo Grocery
⓯ D'Oro Centry Supermarket
⓰ Coop Grocery
⓱ Bike Rental
⓲ Internet Café

limited spots for a fee. When you reserve your room, mention that you'll have a car. Otherwise, try a private lot (about €10-15/half-day, €15-20/24 hours) such as **Autopark,** next to the post office (Via Roma 38, tel. 0185-287-818). An hourly parking lot is by the harbor, in front of the fish market (pay at blue machine with big *Ticket* sign overhead, Mon-Sat 8:00-20:00, Sun 8:00-23:00, first hour-€2, successive hours-€2.50). Parking is generally free where there are white lines; blue lines mean you pay.

Local Guide: Roberta De Beni knows the Ligurian Coast, its history, and its art very well (€100/half-day, €165/day, mobile 349-530-4778, diodebe@inwind.it).

Self-Guided Walk

Welcome to Santa Margherita Ligure

Explore Santa Margherita Ligure on the following stroll.

• *Begin on the water at Piazza della Libertà (just beyond Piazza Veneto). Walk out to the tip of the boat dock and turn around to survey the...*

Town View: From here, you can take in all of Santa Margherita Ligure, from the villas dotting the hills and the castle built in the 16th century (closed except for special exhibitions) to the exclusive hotels. Sharing the dock with you is a statue of "Santa Margherita Virgin Martyr."

• *Wander along the harborfront (down Corso Marconi) past the castle and to the...*

Marina: What's left of the town's fishing fleet ties up here. The fishing industry survives, drag-netting octopus, shrimp, and miscellaneous "blue fish"—plus mountains of anchovies attracted to midnight lamps. The fish market (inside the rust-colored building with arches and columns) wiggles weekdays at about, oh, maybe 16:00-20:00 or so. Residents complain that it's easier to buy their locally caught fresh fish in Milan than here.

• *Head up the flight of narrow brick stairs just to the right of the fish market. At the top stands the...*

Oratory of Sant'Erasmo: This small church is named for St. Erasmus (a.k.a. "St. Elmo"), the protector of sailors. Notice the fine and typically local black-and-white pebble mosaic *(riseu)* in front of the church (with maritime themes). The church is actually an "oratory," where a brotherhood of faithful men who did anonymous good deeds congregated and worshipped. It's decorated with ships and paintings of storms that—thanks to St. Erasmus—the local seafarers survived. The huge crosses standing in the nave are carried through town on special religious holidays (the church is supposedly open only during Mass, but often open at other times, too).

• *With your back to the church, find the loooong stairway (Via Tre Novembre) ahead on the right. Climb it to reach the...*

Church of San Giacomo: Even though this is a secondary church in a secondary town, it's impressively lavish (daily 7:30-19:00, may close earlier in winter, avoid visiting during Mass—usually 7:45-9:00). The region's aristocrats amassed wealth from trade in the 11th to the 15th centuries. When Constantinople fell to the Turks, free trade in the Mediterranean stopped, and Genovese traders became bankers—making even more money. A popular saying of the day was, "Silver is born in America, lives in Spain,

Rise of a Resort: The History of Santa Margherita Ligure

This town, like the entire region (from the border of France to La Spezia), was once ruled by the Republic of Genoa. In the

16th century, when Arab pirates from North Africa plagued the entire coastal area, Genoa built castles in the towns and lookout towers in the neighboring hills.

At the time, Santa Margherita was actually two bickering towns—each with its own bay. In 1800, Napoleon came along, took over the Republic of Genoa, and turned the rival towns into one city—naming it Porto Napoleone. When Napoleon fell in 1815, the town stayed united and took the name of the patron saint of its leading church, Santa Margherita.

In 1850, residents set to work creating a Riviera resort. They imported palm trees from North Africa and paved a fine beach promenade. Santa Margherita (and the surrounding area) was studded with fancy villas built by the aristocracy of Genoa (which was controlled by just 35 families). English, Russian, and German aristocrats also discovered the town in the 19th century. Mass tourism only hit in the last generation. Even with the increased crowds, the town decided to stay chic and kept huge developments out. Its neighbor, Rapallo, chose the extreme opposite—giving the Italian language a new word for uncontrolled growth ruining a once-cute town: *rapallizzazione*.

and dies in Genoa." Bankers here served Spain's 17th-century royalty and aristocracy, and the accrued wealth paid for a Golden Age of art. Wander the church and its chapels, noticing the inlaid-marble floors and sparkling glass chandeliers.

• *Step out of the church and enjoy the sea view. Then turn left and step into...*

Durazzo Park (Parco di Villa Durazzo): This park was an abandoned shambles until 1973, when the city took it over (free, daily 9:00-19:00, off-season until 17:00). Today it's a delight, with a breezy café enjoyed mostly by locals (generally daily from 10:30 except closed Tue May-Aug) and free Wi-Fi (ask at the café for the password). The garden has two distinct parts: the carefully coiffed Italian garden (designed to complement the villa's architecture), and the calculatedly wild "English garden" below. The Italian garden is famous for its varied collection of palm trees and an extensive collection of camellias. It's OK to feed the large turtles in the central pond (they like bits of fish or meat).

• *In the building next to the café, you'll see...*

Villa Durazzo: This was the home of a local journalist and writer, Vittorio G. Rossi (1898-1978), whose office has been preserved as he left it. Typical of the region, this palazzo has some period furniture, several grand pianos, chandeliers, and paintings strewn with cupids on the walls and ceilings. Look for King Umberto's letter offering condolences on Rossi's death. For most people, it's probably not worth the entry fee (€5.50, more for special exhibits; daily 9:00-13:00 & 14:30-18:30, Oct-March until 17:00, last entry 30 minutes before closing, WC opposite entry on left, tel. 0185-293-135, www.villadurazzo.it, villa.durazzo@comunesml.it). Classical music concerts are held here in July and August (ask at TI or villa ticket desk, or call for the schedule).

• *Your self-guided walk is over. Enjoy the park.*

Sights in Santa Margherita Ligure

Basilica of Santa Margherita
(Basilica di Nostra Signora della Rosa)

The town's main church is textbook Italian Baroque. Its 18th-century facade hides a 17th-century interior. The chapels to the right of the high altar contain religious "floats" used in local festival parades. The wooden groups in the niches higher up used to be part of the processions, too. The altar is typical of 17th-century Ligurian altars—shaped like a boat, with lots of shelf space for candles, flowers, and relics. Remember, Baroque is like theater. After the Vatican II decrees of the 1960s, priests began to face their flocks instead of the old altars. For this reason, all over the Catholic world, modern tables serving as post-Vatican II altars stand in front of earlier altars that are no longer the center of attention during the Mass.

Cost and Hours: Free, daily 7:30-12:00 & 15:00-18:30, tel. 0185-286-555.

Via Palestro

This promenade (a.k.a. *caruggio*—"the big street" in local dialect) is *the* strolling street for window-shopping, people-watching, and studying the characteristic Art Nouveau house painting from about 1900. Before 1900, people distinguished their buildings with pastel paint and distinctive door and window frames. Then they decided to get fancy and paint entire exteriors with false balconies, weapons, saints, beautiful women, and 3-D Gothic concentrate.

As you wander from the Basilica of Santa Margherita inland, pop into the fanciest grocer-deli in town—the recommended **Seghezzo** (immediately to the right of the church on Via Cavour).

Locals know that this venerable institution has whatever odd ingredient the most obscure recipe calls for.

Farther up Via Palestro, you might drop into the traditional old **Panificio-Torinese** bakery for a slice of fresh focaccia. Saying "*Vorrei un etto di focaccia*" will get you a Ligurian olive-oily, 100-gram, €1.50 hunk of every kid's favorite beach munchie. Locals claim the best focaccia in Italy is made along this coast.

Markets

On weekday afternoons, fishing boats unload their catch, which is then sold to waiting customers at **Mercato del Pesce** (roughly Mon-Fri 17:00-20:00, opens an hour earlier for wholesalers). Find it in the rust-colored building with arches and columns on Corso Marconi, on the harbor, just past the castle. The open-air market, a commotion of clothes and produce, is held every Friday morning along Corso Matteotti, inland from Piazza Mazzini (8:00-13:00). Piazza Caprera (facing the main church) daily hosts a few farmers selling their produce from stalls.

Beaches

The handiest free Santa Margherita beaches are just below the train station toward the boat dock. But the best beaches are on the south side of town. Among these, I like "Gio and Rino beach" (just before Covo di Nord Est)—not too expensive, with fun, creative management and a young crowd. Also nice is the beach on the south side of Hotel Miramare, which offers a more relaxing sun-worshipping experience. Both beaches have free entry and rentable chairs and umbrellas. They're a 20-minute walk from downtown, or take the bus from either the train station or Piazza Veneto (€1.50 each way if bought in advance from newsstands, tobacco shops, or the green bus ticket kiosk next to the TI; €3 if bought on board).

Paraggi beach, which is halfway to Portofino (with an easy bus connection), is better than any Santa Margherita beach, but it's *very* expensive. One Paraggi beach operator, Bosetti, offers a reasonable rate (€25/day, no hourly rates, includes umbrella, lounge chair, and towel), while rates at other beaches may soar up to €50 per day in July and August. In high season, the Paraggi beach may be all booked up by big shots from Portofino, which has no beach—only rocks. Off-season, the entire Paraggi beach is all yours and free of charge. A skinny patch of sand smack-dab in the middle of Paraggi beach is free year-round.

Sleeping in Santa Margherita Ligure

All of these accommodations are in the center of town. La Locanda di Colombo, Hotel Jolanda, and Hotel Tigullio et de Milan are closest to the station. Prices listed here are the maximum price for the high season of July-August. Expect April-June and September-October to be €10-15 cheaper, and the rest of the year to be cheaper still.

$$$ Hotel Jolanda is a solid, professionally run hotel with 50 rooms, a revolving door, a good breakfast buffet, and a friendly staff. With lavish public spaces and regal colors, this place makes you feel like nobility (Db-€150, superior Db-€170, 10 percent discount if you book directly with the hotel and mention this book when you reserve, air-con, elevator, guest computer, Wi-Fi, free use of small weight room, wet and dry saunas, Jacuzzi, 10 free loaner bikes on request, Via Luisito Costa 6, tel. 0185-287-512, www.hoteljolanda.it, info@hoteljolanda.it).

$$$ Hotel Tigullio et de Milan, run by Giuseppe of Hotel Jolanda, has equally fine rooms with creamy hues and lower prices. You don't get all the luxurious extras, but the breezy sun terrace on top—with a bar in summertime—makes for a relaxing retreat (Db-€140, bigger Db with terrace-€150, 10 percent discount if you book direct with the hotel and mention this book when you reserve, air-con, elevator but lots of stairs down to reception, a few free parking spots, Via Rainusso 3, tel. 0185-287-455, www.hoteltigullio.eu, info@hoteltigullio.eu).

$$$ Hotel Mediterraneo, run by the Melegatti family, offers 30 spacious rooms (a few with balconies or sun terraces) in a family-friendly, creaky, and comfy 18th-century palazzo a five-minute walk from Piazza Veneto. They have a park-like sun garden with lounge chairs and lots of semi-private space. Kindly Pia Pauli presides over the dining room and makes great homemade Ligurian specialties for dinner (Sb-€100, Db-€150, Tb-€180, extensive breakfast, five-course dinner-€30/person, free laundry service with 2-day stay or longer, half the rooms have air-con, Wi-Fi, free parking, free loaner bikes, closed Jan-March, take street immediately to the right of Basilica of Santa Margherita and find hotel straight ahead at Via della Vittoria 18A, tel. 0185-286-881, www.sml-mediterraneo.it, info@sml-mediterraneo.it).

$$$ Hotel Laurin offers slick, modern, air-conditioned, American-style lodgings fixated on harborfront views. All of its 43 rooms face the sea, most have terraces, and there's a small pool on the sundeck, as well as a gym and wet sauna. As it's a Best Western, it feels corporate (Sb-€173, Db-€245, 10 percent discount if you book direct with the hotel and mention this book when you reserve—must show book on arrival, double-paned windows, elevator, 15-yard walk past the castle or €15 taxi ride from station, Corso Marconi 3, tel. 0185-289-971, www.laurinhotel.it, info@ laurinhotel.it).

$$$ Villa Anita is an elegant-yet-homey family hotel run by hospitable Daniela and her friendly son, Sandro. They rent 12 tidy rooms—nearly all with terraces and several with new, high-tech bathrooms—overlooking a peaceful residential neighborhood just a five-minute walk from the seaside boulevard. Daniela makes great cakes, and the in-house chef offers a varying menu of Ligurian specialties (Db-€160, superior Db-€190, dinner-€25/person, family rooms, small heated pool and playground, air-con, free Wi-Fi, free parking, €15 cab ride from station, Viale Minerva 25, tel. 0185-286-543, www.hotelvillaanita.com, info@hotelvillaanita. com).

$$$ Hotel Nuova Riviera is an old villa surrounded by a garden, with nine institutional-feeling rooms, warmly run by the Sabini family (Db-€140, Tb-€160, Qb-€180, 2-night minimum, these prices good in 2014 if you book direct with the hotel and mention this book when you reserve, additional 10 percent discount when you pay cash, fans, some balconies, no elevator, 15-minute walk from station or easy cab ride; if you're driving, follow signs to hospital, then watch for hotel signs on Piazza Mazzini; if you're walking, enter Piazza Mazzini and see signs from there; Via Belvedere 10, tel. 0185-287-403, www.sabinirentals.com, info@sabinirentals.com, chatty Cristina). They also run a nearby annex with six renovated rooms and one apartment with a tiny corner kitchen (Db-€88, Tb-€105, Qb-€125, 2-night minimum, no discounts, cash only, breakfast at Hotel Nuova Riviera is optional and extra, tel. 0185-290-083).

$$$ Hotel Fasce, a 16-room hotel surrounded by flowers and greenery, is run enthusiastically by Florinda and Enrico, whose three kids make this a family-friendly place (Sb-€80, Db-€120, Tb-€150, Qb-€180, two rooms have private bathroom located across the hall, dinner-€20/person, will prepare gluten-free breakfasts, no elevator, free Wi-Fi, free loaner bikes, rooftop garden, laundry service-€15, parking-€20, 10-minute walk or €15 cab ride from station at Via Bozzo 3, tel. 0185-286-435, www.hotelfasce.it, hotelfasce@hotelfasce.it).

Eating in Santa Margherita Ligure

RIVIERA TOWNS

Ristorante "A' Lampara" is the locals' favorite for *casalinga* (home-style) Genovese cuisine, prepared by the endearing Barbieri family: Mamma Maria Luisa oversees the dining room, son Mario cooks, and daughter Natalina serves. Try their specialties, such as *ravioli di pesce*—homemade fish ravioli with red mullet sauce—or *pansotti con salsa di noci*—spinach-stuffed ravioli with walnut sauce (€8-10 pastas, €16-25 *secondi*, Fri-Wed 12:30-14:00 & 19:15-22:00, closed Thu, veggie options, reservations smart for dinner in summer; follow Corso Marconi 4 blocks past the fish market, turn right onto Via Maragliano, and find #33 a block and a half ahead on left; tel. 0185-288-926).

La Cambusa is perched above the culinary heart of Santa Margherita Ligure—the fish market. Popular with tourists and resident romantics, its terrace has an unbeatable view over the harbor. In cooler weather, the terrace is covered and heated. Pick your favorite yacht while tucking into their seafood dishes with a Ligurian twist (€10-13 pasta, €18-22 main dishes, July-Sept daily 9:00-15:00 & 19:00-24:00 except closed Thu morning, Oct-June closed all day Thu, Via T. Bottaro, tel. 0185-287-410; Luciano, wife Antonella, and serious but efficient Vittorio).

Dal Baffo is a bustling mom-and-pop eatery popular for its traditional Ligurian specialties, including homemade pasta, wood-fired pizzas (folks queue up to watch the *pizzaioli* make their €7 pies to go), fresh fish, and grilled steaks at reasonable prices (Wed-Mon 12:00-15:00 & 19:00-23:30, closed Tue; from Piazza Caprera, head inland—both pedestrian streets eventually turn into busy Corso Matteotti; Corso Matteotti 56, tel. 0185-288-987).

Da Pezzi, with a cheap cafeteria-style atmosphere, is packed with locals at midday and at night. They're munching *farinata* (crêpes made from chickpeas, available Oct-May) standing at the bar, or enjoying pesto and fresh fish in the dining room. Consider the deli counter with its Genovese picnic ingredients (Sun-Fri 10:00-14:00 & 17:00-21:00, closed Sat, Via Cavour 21, tel. 0185-285-303, Giancarlo and Giobatta).

Waterfront Dining: All along the harborside of Via Tomaso Bottaro, south of the marina, you'll find restaurants, pizzerias, and bars serving food with a nautical view. **Da Gennaro Pizzeria,** at Piazza della Libertà 30 by the boat dock, makes popular Neapolitan-style pizzas. **Bar Giuli,** the only place actually on the harbor, serves forgettable salads and sandwiches for a reasonable price (about 150 yards south of the fish market, where Via Maragliano meets Via Garibaldi).

Gelato: The best *gelateria* I found in town—with chocolate-truffle *tartufato*—is **Simonetti** (daily 8:30 until late, closed Mon off-season, under the castle, closest to the water at Piazza della Libertà 48). **Gelateria Centrale,** just off Piazza Veneto near the cinema, serves up their specialty—*pinguino* (penguin), a cone with your choice of gelato dipped in chocolate (daily 8:30-late, closed Wed Sept-May).

Groceries: **Seghezzo** is classiest and great for a meal to go—ask them to *riscaldare* (heat up) their white *lasagne al pesto* or dish up their special *carpaccio di polpo*—thinly sliced octopus (daily June-Aug 7:30-13:00 & 15:30-20:00, closed Wed Sept-May, right of the church on Via Cavour, tel. 0185-287-172). The **D'Oro Centry** supermarket, just off Piazza Mazzini at #35, has better prices (Mon-Sat 8:00-13:30 & 15:30-19:30, Sun 8:00-13:00, tel. 0185-286-470), as does the **Co-op** grocery, also off Piazza Mazzini at Corso Giacomo Matteotti 9 (Mon-Sat 8:15-13:00 & 15:30-19:30, Sun 8:30-13:00). Any of these stores is a good place to stock up on well-priced Ligurian olive oil, pasta, and pesto.

Santa Margherita Ligure Connections

From Santa Margherita Ligure by Train to: Sestri Levante (2/hour, 30 minutes), **Monterosso** (at least hourly, 45 minutes), **La Spezia** (hourly, 1-1.5 hours), **Pisa** (1-2/hour, 2-2.5 hours, most connections with transfer, less frequent InterCity/IC goes direct), **Milan** (7/day, 2-2.5 hours, more with transfer in Genoa), **Ventimiglia**/French border (4/day, 4 hours; or hourly with change in Genoa), **Venice** (8/day, 6-7 hours with 1-3 changes). For **Florence,** transfer in Pisa (8/day, 3.5-4 hours).

By Boat to the Cinque Terre: For the latest, pick up a schedule of departures and excursion options from the TI, visit the ticket shack on the dock, call 0185-284-670 or 335-709-0870, or check online at www.traghettiportofino.it. The routes mentioned below run at least once weekly from May through September or October, increasing in frequency in July and August.

"Tour 3" is an all-day trip that includes two stopovers: one hour in Vernazza and three hours in Portovenere, plus a scenic trip around an island (mid-April-Sept departs Sun at 8:45, plus Thu July-Sept, €22 one-way, €33 round-trip).

The half-day "Tour 4" boat sails to the Cinque Terre with a one-hour stopover in Vernazza (July-Sept departs Tue and Fri at 13:30, €17.50 one-way, €25.50 round-trip).

The "Tour 5 Super Cinque Terre" boat offers day-trip cruises from Santa Margherita Ligure to the Cinque Terre, departing at 8:45 and stopping in three Cinque Terre towns: three hours in

Monterosso, and an hour each in Vernazza and Riomaggiore (Wed May-Sept, plus Sat July-Sept, €22 one-way, €33 round-trip).

Portofino

Santa Margherita Ligure, with its aristocratic architecture, hints at old money, whereas nearby Portofino, with its sleek shops, has the sheen of new money. Fortunately, a few pizzerias, *focaccerie*, bars,

and grocery shops are mixed in with Portofino's jewelry shops, art galleries, and haute couture boutiques, making the town affordable. The *piccolo* harbor, classic Italian architecture, and wooded peninsula can turn glitzy Portofino into an appealing package. It makes a fun day trip from Santa Margherita Ligure.

Ever since the Romans founded Portofino for its safe harbor, it has had a strategic value (appreciated by everyone from Napoleon to the Nazis). In the 1950s, *National Geographic* did a beautiful exposé on the idyllic port, and locals claim that's when the Hollywood elite took note. Liz Taylor and Richard Burton came here annually (as did Liz Taylor and Eddie Fisher). During one famous party, Rex Harrison dropped his Oscar into the bay (it was recovered). Ava Gardner came down from her villa each evening for a drink—sporting her famous fur coat. Greta Garbo loved to swim naked in the harbor, not knowing that half the town was watching. Truman Capote also called Portofino home. But VIPs were also here a century earlier. In one of his books, Friedrich Nietzsche wrote about philosophizing with the mythical prophet Zarathustra on the path between Portofino and Santa Margherita.

My favorite Portofino plan: Visit for the evening. Leave Santa Margherita on the bus at about 16:30 and hike the last 20 minutes from Paraggi beach. Explore Portofino. Splurge for a drink on the harborfront, or get a take-out fruity sundae (*paciugo*; pah-CHOO-goh) and sit by the water. Then return by bus to Santa Margherita for dinner (confirm late departures). Portofino offers all kinds of harborside dining, but the quality often doesn't match the high prices. If you do decide to eat in Portofino, **Ristorante lo Stella,** just a few steps from the boat dock, has well-prepared dishes, friendly servers, and portholes in the bathrooms. Opposite the boat dock, little **Solo Gelato** dishes up cones and cups (€3 and up).

Portofino Area

Camogli

To Genoa STATION

To Cinque Terre & Pisa →

Rapallo

PORT

Gulf of Paradise

TUNNEL

See Santa Margherita detail map

TRAIN STATION

BUS STOP B

CHURCH

Santa Margherita Ligure

To Rapallo

BOAT DOCK

Portofino Peninsula

Monte Portofino

TRAIL

GIO & RINO BEACHES

San Fruttuoso

Paraggi

CHRIST OF THE ABYSS

Gulf of Tigullio

Portofino

Ligurian Sea

CASTELLO BROWN

LIGHTHOUSE

Rail
Bus
Trail

1 Kilometer

1 Mile

RIVIERA TOWNS

Getting to Portofino

Portofino makes an easy day trip from Santa Margherita by bus, boat, bike, or foot.

By Bus: Catch bus #82 from Santa Margherita's train station or at bus stops along the harbor (main stop in front of TI, €1.50, 2-3/hour, 15 minutes, goes to Paraggi or Portofino). Buy tickets at the bar next to the train station, at Piazza Veneto's green bus kiosk (next to the TI; daily 7:00-19:30), from the green machine on the side of the kiosk, or at any newsstand, tobacco shop, or shop that displays a *Biglietti Bus* sign. You can usually buy tickets on the bus—for double the cost. If you're at the Piazza Veneto kiosk, grab a bus schedule, which will come in handy if you travel in the evening (last bus around 23:00, #82).

In Portofino, get tickets at the newsstand or tobacco store on Piazza della Libertà, or from the machine next to the bus stop (go uphill from the harbor and you'll come to the piazza—newsstand and tobacco store on the left side; ticket machine and bus stop on the right, directions in English).

By Boat: The boat makes the 15-minute trip with more class and without the traffic jams (€6 one-way, €9 round-trip, €0.50 more on Sun and holidays; nearly hourly departures daily May-Sept 10:15-16:15, Oct-April at 10:15 and 14:15 only; dock is a

2-minute walk from Piazza Veneto off Piazza Martiri della Libertà, call to confirm or pick up schedule from TI or your hotel, tel. 0185-284-670, mobile 336-253-336, check at www.traghettiportofino.it). This company also runs boats from Santa Margherita to the Cinque Terre. The boat from Portofino back to Santa Margherita departs nearly hourly in summer (May-Sept daily 12:00-18:00; Oct-April at 12:00 and 16:00 only).

By Bike: The 25-minute bike ride from Santa Margherita to Portofino is doable for cautious cyclists. While there are no steep hills to struggle up, the road is narrow, with many blind corners. Many of my recommended hotels provide free loaner bikes (though they may not be in the best condition); you can also rent your own wheels.

On Foot: To hike the entire distance from Santa Margherita Ligure to Portofino, you have two options: You can follow the sidewalk along (and sometimes hanging over) the sea (1 hour, 2.5 miles)—although traffic can be noisy, and in places, the footpath disappears. Or, if you're hardy and ambitious, you can take a quieter two-hour hike by leaving Santa Margherita at Via Maragliano, then follow the Ligurian-symbol trail markers (look for red-and-white stripes—they're not always obvious, sometimes numbered according to the path you're on, usually painted on rocks or walls, especially at junctions). This hike takes you high into the hills. Keep left after Cappelletta delle Gave. Several blocks past a castle, you'll drop down into the Paraggi beach, where you'll take the Portofino trail the rest of the way.

Bus and Hike Option: For a shorter hike (20 minutes) into Portofino, ride bus #82 from Santa Margherita only as far as the small but ritzy Paraggi beach. (Ask on board where to get off—watch for an inland bay with green water and a sandy beach.) At the far end of the beach, cross the street, climb the steps, and follow the hilly, paved trail marked *Pedonali per Portofino* high above the road. Twenty minutes later, you'll enter Portofino at a yellow-and-gray-striped church labeled *Divo Martino*—which I figure means "the divine Martin" and has something to do with Dean Martin giving us all "Volare" (which I couldn't get out of my head for the rest of the day).

Orientation to Portofino

Tourist Information: Portofino's TI is uphill from the boat dock and downhill from the bus stop (look for it under a portico—it's on your left coming from the dock, or on your right coming from the bus). Pick up a free town map and a rudimentary hiking map (June-Sept Tue-Sun 10:00-13:00 & 14:00-18:00, closed Mon; Oct-May Tue-Sat 9:30-13:30 & 14:00-17:00, closed Sun-Mon; Via Roma 35, tel. 0185-269-024).

Sights in Portofino

Museo del Parco

For an artsy break, walk around the harbor to the right, where you can stroll around a park littered with 148 contemporary sculptures by mostly Italian artists, including a few top names (€5, June-Oct Wed-Mon 10:00-13:00 & 15:00-19:00, closed Tue, closed Nov-May and in bad weather, mobile 337-333-737, www.museodiportofino.it).

Hikes

One option is the paved stone path that winds up and down to the **lighthouse** *(faro)* at a scenic point with a bar (take the stairs on the right just after Museo del Parco, bar open May-Sept, hedges block views until the end, 25-minute walk). Consider popping into **Castello Brown,** a medieval castle, on the way up or down. It features lush gardens, sweeping viewpoints, and special exhibits about Portofino and its history. Minimal original decorations and exhibits are explained in English (€5, cash only, March-Oct daily 10:00 19:00, Nov-Feb Sat-Sun until 17:00 in winter, tel. 0185-267-101, www.castellobrown.com).

Or you could stroll the hilly pedestrian promenade through the trees from Portofino to **Paraggi beach,** and, if you're lucky, see a wild boar en route (20 minutes, path starts to the right of yellow-and-gray-striped Divo Martino church—look for clock tower, parallels main road, ends at ritzy Paraggi beach, where it's easy to catch bus back to Santa Margherita Ligure).

Another option is to hike out to **San Fruttuoso Abbey** and the nearby underwater Christ statue (described next; the hike there is steep at beginning and end, takes about 2.5 hours from Portofino—pick up the trailhead at the inland-most point of town, past Piazza della Libertà and the *carabinieri* station; you can also hike all the way there from Santa Margherita in about 4.5 hours via Portofino).

The **Parco di Portofino** can provide more information on the many hiking trails that crisscross Portofino's regional parklands (tel. 0185 289-479, www.parcoportofino.it).

Near Portofino

San Fruttuoso Abbey
(Abbazia di San Fruttuoso)

This 11th-century abbey is accessible only by foot (a 2.5-hour hike from Portofino, 4.5 hours from Santa Margherita) or boat (from either Portofino, Santa Margherita, or Camogli; abbey entry-€5, more for special exhibits; June-Sept daily 10:00-17:45; Oct-May daily 10:00-15:45 except closed Mon in winter;

RIVIERA TOWNS

last entry 45 minutes before closing, tel. 0185-772-703, www. fondoambiente.it). But the abbey itself isn't the main attraction. The more intriguing draw is 60 feet underwater, offshore from the abbey, in a specially protected marine area: the statue *Christ of the Abyss (Cristo degli Abissi)*. A boat will take you out to a spot above the statue, where you can look down to just barely see the arms of Jesus—outstretched, reaching upward. Some people bring goggles and dive in for a better view. The statue was placed there in 1954 for the divine protection of the region's divers (€6, trips depart from San Fruttuoso at Sat July-Aug at 15:30, some Mon and Wed sailings—check schedule at www.sopraesottoilmare.net or ask at Portofino TI).

Getting There: The same boats that link Santa Margherita Ligure and Portofino continue on to the San Fruttuoso Abbey (schedule at www.traghettiportofino.it). From Easter through September, a different company's boats continue north from the abbey to Camogli (train station), Recco, and Punta Chiappa (€5-8 one-way, can return to Santa Margherita by train from Camogli or buy round-trip boat tickets, tel. 0185-772-091, schedule at www. golfoparadiso.it). For details inquire at the TI in Portofino or Santa Margherita.

South of the Cinque Terre

La Spezia

While just a quick train ride away from the fanciful Cinque Terre (20-30 minutes), the working town of La Spezia feels like "reality Italy." Primarily a jumping-off point for travelers, the town is slim on sights, and has no beaches.

The pedestrian zone on Via del Prione to the gardens along the harbor makes a pleasant stroll. The nearly deserted **Museo Amedeo Lia** displays Italian paintings from the 13th to 18th centuries, including minor works by Venetian masters Titian, Tintoretto, and Canaletto (€7, Tue-Sun 10:00-18:00, closed Mon, last entry 30 minutes before closing, English descriptions on laminated sheets in most rooms, audioguide-€3, WCs down the hall from ticket desk, 10-minute walk from station at Via del Prione 234, tel. 0187-731-100, http://museolia.spezianet.it).

Stay in the Cinque Terre if you can. But if you're in a bind, I've listed several La Spezia accommodations. I've also listed (under

"Eating in La Spezia") some places to grab a meal while you wait for a train.

Orientation to La Spezia

Tourist Information
The Cinque Terre National Park office is on the platform at track 1 (daily 7:00-21:00, until 19:00 off-season, guest computer-€1.50/20 minutes, tel. 0187-762-600, www.parconazionale5terre.it).

Arrival in La Spezia
By Train: Get off at the La Spezia Centrale stop. You can check your bags at the train station (see "Helpful Hints," next). Exit the station down the road to the left, where several recommended hotels and eateries are located. Another exit takes you out onto Via Fiume by way of the parking garage.

By Car: A handy parking option is under the train station, at the **Park Centro Stazione** (enter from Via Fiume; €1/hour, €6/half-day, about €17/day, or a few euros cheaper with complicated online pre-registration, www.mobpark.it, tel. 0187-187-5303; when returning, punch the code from your ticket into the keypad to open the door). You can park for free at **Piazza d'Armi** (a 20-minute walk to station, or take €1 shuttle bus to Piazza Brin, a 5-minute walk to station; at least 3/hour).

Helpful Hints
Market Days: A colorful covered market sets up in Piazza Cavour (Mon-Sat 7:00-13:00). On Fridays, a huge all-day open-air market sprawls along Viale Garibaldi, about six blocks from the station.

Baggage Storage: A left-luggage service is at the train station along track 1 (facing the tracks on platform 1, go left; it's next to the WC). It's secure, though it isn't always staffed—ring the bell to the left of the doorway to call the attendant. Since you may have to wait, allow plenty of time to pick up your baggage before departing (€3/12 hours, €2 extra per additional 12 hours, daily 8:00-22:00, they'll photocopy your passport).

Laundry: A handy self-service launderette is just below the train station. Head down toward town, and immediately at the first piazza take a sharp right on Via Fiume—it's on your left at #95 (one-hour wash and dry-€8, Mon-Sat 8:30-22:00, Sun 9:00-22:00, mobile 348-543-7924, Edoardo).

Booking Agency: Cinque Terre Riviera books rooms and apartments in La Spezia, the Cinque Terre, and Portovenere for a 10 percent markup.

Getting to the Cinque Terre: Trains leave at least twice hourly for the Cinque Terre, though not all trains stop at all towns. The Cinque Terre Treno Park Card (covers train ride to Cinque Terre as well as hiking fee) is sold at the train-station ticket window and at the national park office in the station (see "Tourist Information," at the beginning of this section). It's also possible to take boat excursions to the Cinque Terre, Portovenere, and outer islands from the La Spezia dock; for current schedules, check at the TI, dock, or www.navigazionegolfodeipoeti.it.

Sleeping in La Spezia

Remember, sleep in La Spezia only as a last resort. These hotels and rooms are within a five-minute walk of La Spezia's station—except the last two listings, which are for drivers only. Prices listed are the high-season rates.

1. Hotel Firenze e Continentale
2. Hotel Astoria
3. Mary Hotel
4. Albergo Parma
5. Casa da Nè/Tre Frè Rooms
6. L'Arca di Noè B&B
7. Ristorante Roma da Marcellin
8. Il Pomodoro Pizzeria
9. Covered Market
10. Launderette
11. Piazza d'Armi (Free Parking)
12. Piazza d'Armi Shuttle Drop-Off
13. Portovenere Bus Stop

RIVIERA TOWNS

Hotels

$$$ Hotel Firenze e Continentale is grand and Old World, but newly restored with a mountain-view breakfast room to boot. Just to the left of the station, its 68 rooms have all the usual comforts (prices vary, but generally Sb-€100, Db-€160, email for best rate, 10 percent discount on best available rate if you book direct with the hotel and mention this book when you reserve, cheaper during slow times, double-paned windows, air-con, elevator, free Wi-Fi, parking in garage-€22/day, Via Paleocapa 7, tel. 0187-713-200, www.hotelfirenzecontinentale.it, info@hotelfirenzecontinentale.it).

$$ Hotel Astoria, with 47 decent rooms, has a combination lobby and breakfast room as large as a school cafeteria. It's a fine backup if the hotels nearer the train station are full (older Db without air-con-€80; Db-€95 for the 10 summery, modern superior rooms with air-con; elevator, free Wi-Fi, free parking in garage—reserve ahead; take Via Milano left of Albergo Parma, go 3 blocks, and turn left to reach Via Roma 139; tel. 0187-714-655, www.albergoastoria.com, info@albergoastoria.com).

$$ Mary Hotel, directly across from the train station, has 48 decent rooms above a big lounge/game room (Sb-€65, Db-€100, air-con, elevator, free Wi-Fi, Via Fiume 177, tel. 0187-743-254, www.hotelmary.it, info@hotelmary.it, friendly Luca).

$$ Albergo Parma, a dumpy last resort with 36 rooms, is a dingy slumbermill, but the price is right (D-€50, Db-€60, breakfast-€4, no fans, free Wi-Fi, some street noise, just below train station and down the stairs at Via Fiume 143, tel. 0187-743-010, www.albergoparma.com, albergoparma@libero.it, Aurelio speaks a bit of English, Silvana doesn't).

Private Rooms

Affitta camera—guesthouses or rented rooms with no official reception—abound near the station. Expect good deals, modest English skills, and no breakfast (buy yourself a coffee and pastry at a nearby bar).

$$ Casa da Nè/Tre Frè has 14 chic rooms with comfy linens and orange trees outside the door. It's located so close to the station that some rooms look out at the tracks; luckily, the windows are double-paned (Db-€80, Tb-€100, Qb-€120, includes breakfast at a café, air-con, free Wi-Fi, Via Paleocapa 4, mobile 347-351-3239, www.trefre.it, info@trefre.it, Paolo).

$$ L'Arca di Noè B&B is homey, with three bright and artsy rooms that offer one of the best deals on the Cinque Terre (one has a bathroom inside the room, while the others have private bathrooms down the hall). A group could take the entire massive apartment (D-€55, Tb-€85, includes breakfast, air-con, communal kitchen, 5-minute walk from station at Via Fiume 39, mobile 320-485-2434, montialessandra@email.it, Alessandra).

Near La Spezia

$$ Il Gelsomino, for drivers only, is a another homey B&B in the hills above La Spezia overlooking the Gulf of Poets. It has three tranquil rooms: one with a bay-view terrace, one with hillside views, and a third that lacks views or a terrace (Db-€70, Tb-€90, Qb-€110, reconfirm several days in advance with your arrival time, large breakfast, Via dei Viseggi 9, tel. 0187-704-201, www.ilgelsomino.biz, ilgelsomino@inwind.it, gracious Carla and Walter Massi). Don't confuse this B&B with the one named Il Gelsomino d'Oro.

$ Santa Maria del Mare Monastery, a last resort for drivers, rents 15 comfortable rooms to spiritual travelers high above La Spezia in a scenic but institutional setting (donation only, recommended offerings: dorm bed-€35, Db-€60, includes breakfast, additional €15/person for a meal, Via Montalbano 135B, tel.

0187-711-382, , mobile 347-848-3993, www.santamariadelmare.it, madre@santamariadelmare.191.it).

Eating in La Spezia

Ristorante Roma da Marcellin, a one-minute walk from the station, has a cool, leafy terrace that's ideal for relaxing while you await your train. Grandpa Ottorino cooks up the freshest catch, as well as homemade ravioli and spaghetti *frutti di mare* (€8-12 pastas, €9-15 *secondi*, daily 12:15-15:00 & 19:30-23:00; as you exit the station, turn left—it's across from Hotel Firenze e Continentale at Via Paleocapa 18; tel. 0187-715-921).

Il Pomodoro Pizzeria, just a few doors farther down on the corner of Via Zampino, offers more reasonable prices and an extensive selection of €6-8 pizzas. Practice your Italian with the chalkboard display of pastas of the day (Mon-Fri 12:00-14:00 & 19:00-23:00, Sat 19:00-23:00, closed Sun, Piazza S. Bon 5, tel. 0187-739-911).

La Spezia Connections

From La Spezia by Train to: Monterosso (2-3/hour, 15-30 minutes, €2.60), **Carrara** (2/hour, 25 minutes, €2.40), **Viareggio** (2/hour, 30-60 minutes, €4), **Pisa** (hourly, 1-1.5 hours, €5-9), **Florence** (4/day direct, otherwise nearly hourly, 2.5 hours, change in Pisa, €9), **Rome** (every 2 hours, 3.5-5 hours, €35-45), **Milan** (about hourly, 3 hours direct or with change in Genoa, €22-29), **Venice** (nearly hourly, 5 hours, 1-3 changes, €50-55).

By Bus to Portovenere: City buses generally depart from Viale Garibaldi (bus #P, 2/hour, 30 minutes, €2.50 each way; bus #11 also makes this trip, but only mid-June-mid-Sept and off-season Sat; buy tickets at tobacco shops or newsstands). From the La Spezia train station, exit left and head downhill, following the street to the first square (Piazza S. Bon). Continue down the pedestrian stretch of Via Fiume to Piazza Garibaldi, then turn right at the fountain in the square onto Viale Garibaldi; the bus stop for Portovenere-bound buses is after the first stoplight on the right side of the street. A timetable is posted by the bus stop.

Carrara

What are perhaps the world's most famous marble quarries are just east of La Spezia in Carrara. Michelangelo himself traveled to these valleys to pick out the marble that he would work into his masterpieces. The towns of the region are dominated by marble. The quarries higher up are vast digs that dwarf the hardworking trucks and machinery coming and going. The **Marble Museum** (Museo Civico del Marmo) traces the story of marble-cutting here from pre-Roman times until today (€4.50, May-Sept Mon-Sat 9:30-13:00 & 15:30-18:00, Oct-April Mon-Sat 9:00-12:30 & 14:30-17:00, closed Sun year-round, Viale XX Settembre 85, tel. 0585-845-746, www.museodelmarmo.com).

For a guided visit, **Sara Paolini** is excellent (€80/half-day tour, mobile 373-711-6695, sarapaolini@hotmail.com). She is accustomed to meeting drivers at the Carrara freeway exit, or she can pick you up at the train station.

Portovenere

While the gritty port of La Spezia offers little in the way of redeeming touristic value, the nearby resort of Portovenere is enchanting. This Cinque Terre-esque village clings to a rocky promontory that juts into the sea and protects the harbor from the crashing waves. On the harbor, next to colorful bobbing boats, a row of restaurants—perfect for al fresco dining—feature local specialties such as *trenette* pasta with pesto and *spaghetti con frutti di mare.*

Local boats take you on a 40-minute excursion around three nearby islands or over to Lerici, the town across the bay. Lord Byron swam to Lerici (not recommended). Hardy hikers enjoy the five-hour (or more) hike to Riomaggiore, the nearest Cinque Terre town.

Getting There: Portovenere—not to be confused with Portofino—is an easy day trip from the Cinque Terre by **boat** (mid-

June-Oct, 4-6/day, 1 hour, €13 one-way, €25 day pass includes hopping on and off and either Lerici or a jaunt around three small islands near Portovenere, www.navigazionegolfodeipoeti.it). You can also cruise between Portovenere and Santa Margherita Ligure, with stops in Vernazza and Sestri Levante, using another boat line (www.traghettiportofino.it). Pick up a schedule of departures and excursion options from the TI, or ask at your hotel. Or you can take the **bus** from La Spezia (bus #P, 2/hour, 30 minutes, €2.50 each way; bus #11 also makes this trip, but only mid-June-mid-Sept and off-season Sat; in La Spezia buy tickets at tobacco shops or news-stands; in Portovenere get tickets at TI). **Parking** is a nightmare here from May through September, but Albergo Il Genio offers free parking. In peak season, buses shuttle drivers from the parking lot just outside Portovenere to the harborside square. Otherwise, test your luck with the spots on the seaside (€2/hour).

Tourist Information: The TI is easy to find in the main square (daily June-Sept 10:00-12:00 & 15:00-19:45; Oct-May Thu-Tue 10:00-12:00 & 15:00-18:00, closed Wed; Piazza Bastreri 7, tel. 0187-790-691, www.prolocoportovenere.it).

Sleeping in Portovenere: If you've forgotten your yacht, try **$$$ Albergo Il Genio,** in the building where the main street hits the piazza (Db-€100, Qb-€130, some rooms with views, no el-evator, guest computer, free parking but request when you reserve, Piazza Bastreri 8, tel. 0187-790-611, www.hotelgenioportovenere.com, info@hotelgenioportovenere.com).

PRACTICALITIES

This section covers just the basics on traveling in Italy (for much more information, see *Rick Steves' Italy*). You can find free advice on specific topics at www.ricksteves.com/tips.

Money

Italy uses the euro currency: 1 euro (€) = about $1.30. To convert prices in euros to dollars, add about 30 percent: €20 = about $26, €50 = about $65. (Check www.oanda.com for the latest exchange rates.)

The standard way for travelers to get euros is to withdraw money from ATMs (which locals call a *bancomat*) using a debit or credit card, ideally with a Visa or MasterCard logo. Before departing, call your bank or credit-card company: Confirm that your card will work overseas, ask about international transaction fees, and alert them that you'll be making withdrawals in Europe. Also ask for the PIN number for your credit card in case it'll help you use Europe's "chip-and-PIN" payment machines (see below); allow time for your bank to mail your PIN to you. To keep your valuables safe while traveling, wear a money belt.

Dealing with "Chip and PIN": Much of Europe (including Italy) is adopting a "chip-and-PIN" system for credit cards, and some merchants rely on it exclusively. European chip-and-PIN cards are embedded with an electronic chip, in addition to the magnetic stripe used on our American-style cards. This means that your credit (and debit) card might not work at automated payment machines, such as those at train and subway stations, toll roads, parking garages, luggage lockers, and self-serve gas pumps. Memorizing your credit card's PIN lets you use it at some chip-and-PIN machines—just enter your PIN when prompted. If a payment machine won't take your card, look for a machine that takes cash or see if there's a cashier nearby who can process your transaction. The easiest solution is to pay for your purchases with cash you've withdrawn from an ATM using your debit card (Europe's ATMs still accept magnetic-stripe cards).

Phoning

Smart travelers use the telephone to reserve or reconfirm rooms, reserve restaurants, get directions, research transportation connections, confirm tour times, phone home, and lots more.

To call Italy from the US or Canada: Dial 011-39 and then the local number. (The 011 is our international access code, and 39 is Italy's country code.)

To call Italy from a European country: Dial 00-39 followed by the local number. (The 00 is Europe's international access code.)

To call within Italy: Just dial the local number.

To call from Italy to another country: Dial 00 followed by the country code (for example, 1 for the US or Canada), then the area code and number. If you're calling European countries whose phone numbers begin with 0, you'll usually have to omit that 0 when you dial.

Tips on Phoning: A mobile phone—whether an American one that works in Italy, or a European one you buy when you arrive—is handy, but can be pricey. If traveling with a smartphone, switch off data-roaming until you have free Wi-Fi. If you have a smartphone, you can use it to make free or inexpensive calls in Europe by using a calling app such as Skype or FaceTime when you're on Wi-Fi.

To make cheap international calls from any phone (even your hotel-room phone), you can buy an international phone card in Italy. These work with a scratch-to-reveal PIN code, allow you to call home to the US for pennies a minute, and also work for domestic calls.

Another option is buying an insertable phone card in Italy. These are usable only at pay phones, are reasonable for making calls within the country, and work for international calls as well (though not as cheaply as the international phone cards). Note that insertable phone cards—and most international phone cards—work only in the country where you buy them.

Calling from your hotel-room phone is usually expensive, unless you use an international phone card. For more on phoning, see www.ricksteves.com/phoning.

Making Hotel Reservations

To ensure the best value, I recommend reserving rooms in advance, particularly during peak season. Email the hotelier with the following key pieces of information: number and type of rooms;

From:	rick@ricksteves.com
Sent:	Today
To:	info@hotelcentral.com
Subject:	Reservation request for 19-22 July

Dear Hotel Central,

I would like to reserve a double room for 2 people for 3 nights, arriving 19 July and departing 22 July. If possible, I would like a quiet room with a bathroom inside the room.

Please let me know if you have a room available and the price.

Thank you!
Rick Steves

number of nights; date of arrival; date of departure; and any special requests. (For a sample form, see sidebar above.) Use the European style for writing dates: day/month/year. For example, for a two-night stay in July, you could request: "1 double room for 2 nights, arrive 16/07/14, depart 18/07/14." Hoteliers typically ask for your credit-card number as a deposit.

Given the economic downturn, hoteliers are often willing and eager to make a deal—try emailing several to ask their best price. In general, hotel prices can soften if you do any of the following: offer to pay cash, stay at least three nights, or mention this book. You can also try asking for a cheaper room or a discount, or offer to skip breakfast.

Eating

Italy offers a wide array of eateries. A *ristorante* is a formal restaurant, while a *trattoria* or *osteria* is usually more traditional and simpler (but can still be pricey). Italian "bars" are not taverns, but small cafés selling sandwiches, coffee, and other drinks. An *enoteca* is a wine bar with snacks and light meals. Take-away food from pizza shops and delis (such as a *rosticcería* or *tavola calda*) makes an easy picnic.

Italians eat dinner a bit later than we do; better restaurants start serving around 19:00. A full meal consists of an appetizer (antipasto), a first course (*primo piatto,* pasta, rice, or soup), and a second course (*secondo piatto,* expensive meat and fish/seafood dishes). Vegetables *(verdure)* may come with the *secondo,* but more often must be ordered separately as a side dish (*contorno*). Desserts (*dolci*) can be very tempting. The euros can add up in a hurry, but you don't have to order each course. My approach is to mix antipasti and *primi piatti* family-style with my dinner partners (skipping *secondi*). Or, for a basic value, look for a *menù del giorno,* a three- or four-course, fixed-price meal deal (avoid the cheapest ones, often called a *menù turistico*).

Good service is relaxed (slow to an American). You won't get the bill until you ask for it: *"Il conto?"* Most restaurants include a service charge in their prices (check the menu for *servizio incluso*—generally around 15 percent). To reward good service, add a euro or two for each person in your party. If you order at a counter rather than from waitstaff, there's no need to tip. Many (but not all) restaurants in Italy add a cover charge *(coperto)* of €1-3.50 per person to your bill.

At bars and cafés, getting a drink while standing at the bar *(banco)* is cheaper than drinking it at a table *(tavolo)* or sitting outside *(terrazza)*. This tiered pricing system is clearly posted on the wall. Sometimes you'll pay at a cash register, then take the receipt to another counter to claim your drink.

Transportation

By Train: In Italy, most travelers find it's cheapest simply to buy train tickets as they go. To see if a railpass could save you money, check www.ricksteves.com/rail. To research train schedules, visit Germany's excellent all-Europe website, www.bahn.com, or Italy's www.trenitalia.com. A private company called Italo is also running fast trains on major routes in Italy; see www.italotreno.it.

You can buy tickets at train stations (at the ticket window or at automated machines with English instructions) or from travel agencies. Before boarding the train, you must validate your train documents by stamping them in the machine near the platform (usually marked *convalida biglietti* or *vidimazione*). Strikes *(sciopero)* are common and generally announced in advance (but a few sporadic trains still run—ask around).

By Car: It's cheaper to arrange most car rentals from the US. For tips on your insurance options, see www.ricksteves.com/cdw, and for route planning, consult www.viamichelin.com. Theft insurance is mandatory in Italy ($15-20/day). Bring your driver's license. You're also technically required to have an International Driving Permit (sold at your local AAA office for $15 plus the cost of two passport-type photos; see www.aaa.com).

Italy's freeway *(autostrada)* system is slick and speedy, but you'll pay about a dollar for every 10 minutes of use. Be warned that car traffic is restricted in many city centers—don't drive or park in any area that has a sign reading *Zona Traffico Limitato* (*ZTL*, often shown above a red circle)...or you might be mailed a ticket later.

Local road etiquette is similar to that in the US. Ask your car-rental company about the rules of the road, or check the US State Department website (www.travel.state.gov, click on "International Travel," then specify your country of choice and click "Traffic Safety and Road Conditions").

A car is a worthless headache in cities—park it safely (get tips from your hotel). As break-ins are common, be sure all of your valuables are out of sight and locked in the trunk, or even better, with you or in your hotel room.

Helpful Hints

Emergency Help: For English-speaking **police** help, dial 113. To summon an **ambulance**, call 118. For passport problems, call the **US Embassy** (in Rome, 24-hour line—tel. 06-46741) or **US Consulates** (Milan—tel. 02-290-351, Florence—tel. 055-266-951, Naples—tel. 081-583-8111); or the **Canadian Embassy** (in Rome, tel. 06-854-441). For other concerns, get advice from your hotelier.

Theft or Loss: Italy has particularly hardworking pickpockets—wear a money belt. Assume beggars are pickpockets and any scuffle is simply a distraction by a team of thieves. If you stop for any commotion or show, put your hands in your pockets before someone else does.

To replace a passport, you'll need to go in person to an embassy or consulate (see above). Cancel and replace your credit and debit cards by calling these 24-hour US numbers collect: Visa—tel. 303/967-1096, MasterCard—tel. 636/722-7111, American Express—tel. 336/393-1111. File a police report either on the spot or within a day or two; you'll need it to submit an insurance claim for lost or stolen railpasses or travel gear, and it can help with replacing your passport or credit and debit cards. Precautionary measures can minimize the effects of loss—back up your digital photos and other files frequently. For more information, see www.ricksteves.com/help.

Time: Italy uses the 24-hour clock. It's the same through 12:00 noon, then keep going: 13:00, 14:00, and so on. Italy, like most of continental Europe, is six/nine hours ahead of the East/West Coasts of the US.

Business Hours: Many businesses have now adopted the government's recommended 8:00 to 14:00 workday (although in tourist areas, shops are open longer). Still, expect small towns and villages to be more or less shut tight during the midafternoon. Stores are also usually closed on Sunday, and often on Monday.

Sights: Opening and closing hours of sights can change unexpectedly; confirm the latest times with the local tourist information office or its website. Some major churches enforce a modest dress code (no bare shoulders or shorts) for everyone, even children.

Holidays and Festivals: Italy celebrates many holidays, which can close sights and attract crowds (book hotel rooms ahead). For information on holidays and festivals, check Italy's website: www.italia.it. For a simple list showing major—though not all—events, see www.ricksteves.com/festivals.

Numbers and Stumblers: What Americans call the second floor of a building is the first floor in Europe. Europeans write dates as day/month/year, so Christmas is 25/12/14. Commas are decimal points and vice versa—a dollar and a half is 1,50, and there are 5.280 feet in a mile. Italy uses the metric system: A kilogram is 2.2 pounds; a liter is about a quart; and a kilometer is six-tenths of a mile.

Resources from Rick Steves

This Snapshot guide is excerpted from my latest edition of *Rick Steves' Italy*, which is one of more than 30 titles in my series of guidebooks on European travel. I also produce a public television series, *Rick Steves' Europe*, and a public radio show, *Travel with Rick Steves*. My website, www.ricksteves.com, offers free travel information, a Graffiti Wall for travelers' comments, guidebook updates, my travel blog, an online travel store, and information on European railpasses and our tours of Europe. If you're bringing a mobile device on your trip, you can download free information from Rick Steves Audio Europe, featuring podcasts of my radio shows, free audio tours of major sights in Europe, and travel interviews about Italy (via www.ricksteves.com/audioeurope, iTunes, Google Play, or the Rick Steves Audio Europe free smartphone app). You can follow me on Facebook and Twitter.

Additional Resources

Tourist Information: www.italia.it
Passports and Red Tape: www.travel.state.gov
Travel Insurance Tips: www.ricksteves.com/insurance
Packing List: www.ricksteves.com/packlist
Cheap Flights: www.kayak.com
Airplane Carry-on Restrictions: www.tsa.gov/travelers
Updates for This Book: www.ricksteves.com/update

How Was Your Trip?

If you'd like to share your tips, concerns, and discoveries after using this book, please fill out the survey at www.ricksteves.com/feedback. Thanks in advance—it helps a lot.

Italian Survival Phrases

English	Italian	Pronunciation
Good day.	Buon giorno.	bwohn **jor**-noh
Do you speak English?	Parla inglese?	**par**-lah een-**glay**-zay
Yes. / No.	Sì. / No.	see / noh
I (don't) understand.	(Non) capisco.	(nohn) kah-**pees**-koh
Please.	Per favore.	pehr fah-**voh**-ray
Thank you.	Grazie.	**graht**-seeay
You're welcome.	Prego.	**pray**-go
I'm sorry.	Mi dispiace.	mee dee-**speeah**-chay
Excuse me.	Mi scusi.	mee **skoo**-zee
(No) problem.	(Non) c'è un problema.	(nohn) cheh oon proh-**blay**-mah
Good.	Va bene.	vah **behn**-ay
Goodbye.	Arrivederci.	ah-ree-vay-**dehr**-chee
one / two	uno / due	**oo**-noh / **doo**-ay
three / four	tre / quattro	tray / **kwah**-troh
five / six	cinque / sei	**cheeng**-kway / **se**hee
seven / eight	sette / otto	**seht**-tay / **ot**-toh
nine / ten	nove / dieci	**nov**-ay / **deeay**-chee
How much is it?	Quanto costa?	**kwahn**-toh **kos**-tah
Write it?	Me lo scrive?	may loh **skree**-vay
Is it free?	È gratis?	eh **grah**-tees
Is it included?	È incluso?	eh een-**kloo**-zoh
Where can I buy / find...?	Dove posso comprare / trovare...?	**doh**-vay **pos**-soh kohm-**prah**-ray / troh-**vah**-ray
I'd like / We'd like...	Vorrei / Vorremmo...	vor-**rehee** / vor-**ray**-moh
...a room.	...una camera.	**oo**-nah **kah**-meh-rah
...a ticket to ____.	...un biglietto per ____.	oon beel-**yeht**-toh pehr
Is it possible?	È possibile?	eh poh-**see**-bee-lay
Where is...?	Dov'è...?	**doh**-veh
...the train station	...la stazione	lah staht-seeoh-nay
...the bus station	...la stazione degli autobus	lah staht-seeoh-nay **dayl**-yee **ow**-toh-boos
...tourist information	...informazioni per turisti	een-for-maht-seeoh-nee pehr too-**ree**-stee
...the toilet	...la toilette	lah twah-**leht**-tay
men	uomini, signori	**woh**-mee-nee, seen-**yoh**-ree
women	donne, signore	**don**-nay, seen-**yoh**-ray
left / right	sinistra / destra	see-**nee**-strah / **dehs**-trah
straight	sempre diritto	**sehm**-pray dee-**ree**-toh
When do you open / close?	A che ora aprite / chiudete?	ah kay **oh**-rah ah-**pree**-tay / keeoo-**day**-tay
At what time?	A che ora?	ah kay **oh**-rah
Just a moment.	Un momento.	oon moh-**mayn**-toh
now / soon / later	adesso / presto / tardi	ah-**dehs**-soh / **prehs**-toh / **tar**-dee
today / tomorrow	oggi / domani	**oh**-jee / doh-**mah**-nee

In an Italian-speaking Restaurant

English	Italian	Pronunciation
I'd like...	Vorrei...	vor-**rehee**
We'd like...	Vorremmo...	vor-**ray**-moh
...to reserve...	...prenotare...	pray-noh-**tah**-ray
...a table for one / two.	...un tavolo per uno / due.	oon **tah**-voh-loh pehr **oo**-noh / **doo**-ay
Non-smoking.	Non fumare.	nohn foo-**mah**-ray
Is this seat free?	È libero questo posto?	eh **lee**-bay-roh **kwehs**-toh **poh**-stoh
The menu (in English), please.	Il menù (in inglese), per favore.	eel may-**noo** (een een-**glay**-zay) pehr fah-**voh**-ray
service (not) included	servizio (non) incluso	sehr-**veet**-seeoh (nohn) een-**kloo**-zoh
cover charge	pane e coperto	**pah**-nay ay koh-**pehr**-toh
to go	da portar via	dah **por**-tar **vee**-ah
with / without	con / senza	kohn / **sehn**-sah
and / or	e / o	ay / oh
menu (of the day)	menù (del giorno)	may-**noo** (dayl **jor**-noh)
specialty of the house	specialità della casa	spay-chah-lee-**tah dehl**-lah **kah**-zah
first course (pasta, soup)	primo piatto	**pree**-moh peeah-toh
main course (meat, fish)	secondo piatto	say-**kohn**-doh peeah-toh
side dishes	contorni	kohn-**tor**-nee
bread	pane	**pah**-nay
cheese	formaggio	for-**mah**-joh
sandwich	panino	pah-**nee**-noh
soup	minestra, zuppa	mee-**nehs**-trah, **tsoo**-pah
salad	insalata	een-sah-**lah**-tah
meat	carne	**kar**-nay
chicken	pollo	**poh**-loh
fish	pesce	**peh**-shay
seafood	frutti di mare	**froo**-tee dee **mah**-ray
fruit / vegetables	frutta / legumi	**froo**-tah / lay-**goo**-mee
dessert	dolci	**dohl**-chee
tap water	acqua del rubinetto	**ah**-kwah dayl roo-bee-**nay**-toh
mineral water	acqua minerale	**ah**-kwah mee-nay-**rah**-lay
milk	latte	**lah**-tay
(orange) juice	succo (d'arancia)	**soo**-koh (dah-**rahn**-chah)
coffee / tea	caffè / tè	kah-**feh** / teh
wine	vino	**vee**-noh
red / white	rosso / bianco	**roh**-soh / beeahn-koh
glass / bottle	bicchiere / bottiglia	bee-keeay-ray / boh-**teel**-yah
beer	birra	**bee**-rah
Cheers!	Cin cin!	cheen cheen
More. / Another.	Ancora un po.' / Un altro.	ahn-**koh**-rah oon poh / oon **ahl**-troh
The same.	Lo stesso.	loh **stehs**-soh
The bill, please.	Il conto, per favore.	eel **kohn**-toh pehr fah-**voh**-ray
tip	mancia	**mahn**-chah
Delicious!	Delizioso!	day-leet-seeoh-zoh

For more user-friendly Italian phrases, check out *Rick Steves' Italian Phrase Book & Dictionary* or *Rick Steves' French, Italian, and German Phrase Book.*

PRACTICALITIES

INDEX

Audio Europe™

Rick's Free Travel App

Get your FREE **Rick Steves Audio Europe**™ app to enjoy...

- Dozens of self-guided tours of Europe's top museums, sights and historic walks

- Hundreds of tracks filled with cultural insights and sightseeing tips from Rick's radio interviews

- All organized into handy geographic playlists

- For iPhone, iPad, iPod Touch, Android

With Rick whispering in your ear, Europe gets even better.

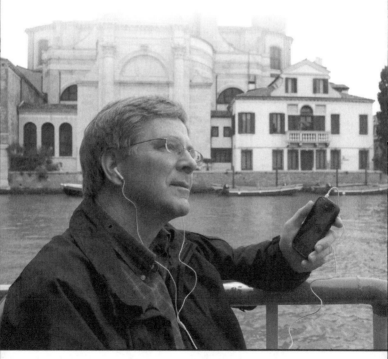

Find out more at ricksteves.com

Start your trip at

Free information and great gear to

▶ Explore Europe

Browse thousands of articles, video clips, photos and radio interviews, plus find a wealth of money-saving tips for planning your dream trip. You'll find up-to-date information on Europe's best destinations, packing smart, getting around, finding rooms, staying healthy, avoiding scams and more.

▶ Travel News

Subscribe to our free Travel News e-newsletter, and get monthly updates from Rick on what's happening in Europe!

▶ Travel Forums

Learn, ask, share—our online community of savvy travelers is a great resource for first-time travelers to Europe, as well as seasoned pros.

Rick Steves' Europe Through the Back Door, Inc

ricksteves.com

turn your travel dreams into affordable reality

▶ Rick's Free Audio Europe™ App

The Rick Steves Audio Europe™ app brings history and art to life. Enjoy Rick's audio tours of Europe's top museums, sights and neighborhood walks—plus hundreds of tracks including travel tips and cultural insights from Rick's radio show—all organized into geographic playlists. Learn more at ricksteves.com.

▶ Great Gear from Rick's Travel Store

Pack light and right—on a budget—with Rick's custom-designed carry-on bags, wheeled bags, day packs, travel accessories, guidebooks, journals, maps and Blu-ray/DVDs of his TV shows.

130 Fourth Avenue North, PO Box 2009 • Edmonds, WA 98020 USA
Phone: (425) 771-8303 • Fax: (425) 771-0833 • ricksteves.com

NOW AVAILABLE:
eBOOKS, DVD & BLU-RAY

TRAVEL CULTURE

Europe 101
European Christmas
Postcards from Europe
Travel as a Political Act

eBOOKS

*Nearly all Rick Steves guides
are available as eBooks. Check
with your favorite bookseller.*

RICK STEVES' EUROPE DVDs

11 New Shows 2013–2014
Austria & the Alps
Eastern Europe
England & Wales
European Christmas
European Travel Skills & Specials
France
Germany, BeNeLux & More
Greece, Turkey & Portugal
Iran
Ireland & Scotland
Italy's Cities
Italy's Countryside
Scandinavia
Spain
Travel Extras

BLU-RAY

Celtic Charms
Eastern Europe Favorites
European Christmas
Italy Through the Back Door
Mediterranean Mosaic
Surprising Cities of Europe

PHRASE BOOKS & DICTIONARIES

French
French, Italian & German
German
Italian
Portuguese
Spanish

JOURNALS

Rick Steves' Pocket Travel Journal
Rick Steves' Travel Journal

PLANNING MAPS

Britain, Ireland & London
Europe
France & Paris
Germany, Austria & Switzerland
Ireland
Italy
Spain & Portugal

Rick Steves books and DVDs are available at bookstores
and through online booksellers.

Rick Steves

EUROPE GUIDES

Best of Europe
Eastern Europe
Europe Through the Back Door
Mediterranean Cruise Ports
Northern European Cruise Ports

COUNTRY GUIDES

Croatia & Slovenia
England
France
Germany
Great Britain
Ireland
Italy
Portugal
Scandinavia
Spain
Switzerland

CITY & REGIONAL GUIDES

Amsterdam, Bruges & Brussels
Barcelona
Budapest
Florence & Tuscany
Greece: Athens & the Peloponnese
Istanbul
London
Paris
Prague & the Czech Republic
Provence & the French Riviera
Rome
Venice
Vienna, Salzburg & Tirol

SNAPSHOT GUIDES

Berlin
Bruges & Brussels
Copenhagen & the Best of
    Denmark
Dublin
Dubrovnik
Hill Towns of Central Italy
Italy's Cinque Terre
Krakow, Warsaw & Gdansk
Lisbon
Madrid & Toledo
Milan & the Italian Lakes District
Munich, Bavaria & Salzburg
Naples & the Amalfi Coast
Northern Ireland
Norway
Scotland
Sevilla, Granada & Southern Spain
Stockholm

POCKET GUIDES

Athens
Barcelona
Florence
London
Paris
Rome
Venice

Avalon Travel
a member of the Perseus Books Group
1700 Fourth Street
Berkeley, CA 94710

Printed in Canada by Friesens
First printing January 2014

ISBN 978-1-61238-685-0

For the latest on Rick's lectures, guidebooks, tours, public radio show, and public television series, contact Europe Through the Back Door, Box 2009, Edmonds, WA 98020, tel. 425/771-8303, fax 425/771-0833, www.ricksteves.com, rick@ricksteves.com.

Europe Through the Back Door

Managing Editor: Risa Laib
Editorial & Production Manager: Jennifer Madison Davis
Editors: Glenn Eriksen, Tom Griffin, Cameron Hewitt, Suzanne Kotz, Cathy Lu, Carrie Shepherd, Gretchen Strauch
Editorial Assistant: Jessica Shaw
Editorial Intern: Alex Jacobs
Researchers: Ben Cameron, Cameron Hewitt, Helen Inman, Suzanne Kotz, Marijan Kriskovic, Cary Walker, Ian Watson
Maps & Graphics: David C. Hoerlein, Lauren Mills, Dawn Tessman Visser, Laura VanDeventer

Avalon Travel

Senior Editor and Series Manager: Madhu Prasher
Editor: Jamie Andrade
Associate Editor: Annette Kohl
Assistant Editor: Maggie Ryan
Copy Editor: Jennifer Malnick
Proofreader: Suzie Nasol
Indexer: Stephen Callahan
Cover Design: Kimberly Glyder Design
Maps & Graphics: Kat Bennett, Mike Morgenfeld

Front Cover Photo: Manarola village, Cinque Terre, Italy © Borut Trdina / istockphoto.com
Additional Photography: Dominic Bonuccelli, Ben Cameron, Jennifer Hauseman, Cameron Hewitt, David C. Hoerlein, Anne Jenkins, Gene Openshaw, Michael Potter, Robyn Stencil, Rick Steves, Bruce VanDeventer, Laura VanDeventer, Les Wahlstrom, Ian Watson, Wikimedia Commons

ABOUT THE AUTHOR

RICK STEVES

Since 1973, Rick Steves has spent 100 days every year exploring Europe. Along with writing and researching a bestselling series of guidebooks, Rick produces a public television series *(Rick Steves' Europe)*, a public radio show *(Travel with Rick Steves)*, and an app and podcast *(Rick Steves Audio Europe)*; writes a nationally syndicated newspaper column; organizes guided tours that take over ten thousand travelers to Europe annually; and offers an information-packed website (www.ricksteves.com). With the help of his hardworking staff of 80 at Europe Through the Back Door—in Edmonds, Washington, just north of Seattle—Rick's mission is to make European travel fun, affordable, and culturally enlightening for Americans.

Connect with Rick:

facebook.com/RickSteves   twitter: @RickSteves

Want More Italy?
Maximize the experience with Rick Steves as your guide

Guidebooks
Venice, Florence, and Rome guides make side-trips smooth and affordabl

Phrase Books
Rely on Rick's Italian Phrase Book and Dictionary

Rick's DVDs
Preview where you're going with 15 shows on Italy

Free! Rick's Audio Europe™ App
Get free audio tours for Italy's top sights

Small-Group Tours
Rick offers a dozen great itineraries through Italy

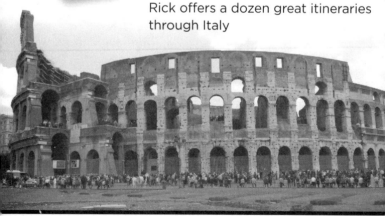